AN
GUIDE TO

THE
LAKE DISTRICT

by

James Holgate

and

Geoff Parkinson

Westmorland Gazette, Kendal, Cumbria.

First published 1985
Second edition 1987
Third edition 1988

© Westmorland Gazette

ISBN 0 902272 69 1

Published by
Westmorland Gazette, 22 Stricklandgate,
Kendal, Cumbria.

Printed by
Titus Wilson & Son Ltd., Redmaynes Yard,
Kendal, Cumbria.

FOREWORD

It would be hard for any keen angler to look at a map of the Lake District without his or her eyes immediately focusing on all those alluring patches of blue with which the region is dotted. Yet it's surprising that, in an area which actually derives its name from the abundance of lakes and tarns within its boundaries, up to the present there has been no single book which deals comprehensively with angling facilities in these waters. This is an omission which we hope to have remedied by this publication.

So what will angler's who make use of the information in these pages find? Well, you will most certainly experience a great deal of variety in the circumstances in which you fish. For example, go and fish a water like Windermere on a sunny bank holiday, and the Lake District will seem a very crowded place indeed. On the other hand, try fishing a small remote water like Beacon Tarn in the depths of winter, and it is equally possible to find the true meaning of the word solitude.

Although there is a lot of water to fish, this is not, in most of the lakes, matched by a large variety of indigenous species. As a general rule, trout (brown, although an increasing number of rainbows are being stocked), salmon, sea trout, pike and perch, will be angler's main quarry. There are also three more unusual species in some of the lakes, charr, schelly, and vendace, which we will mention as the occasion arises, along with other species present.

When starting to write this book, we both resolved to make it as comprehensive as possible. As a result, we have tried to include as many waters as we could, both in and around Lakeland. We may not have succeeded in tracking down every duck pond, but we did at least try!

We would advise that if you are thinking of really exploring the Lake District's angling potential, you should purchase a good quality Ordnance Survey map of the area, on which all the waters featured in this guide will be shown.

As you will see in the following chapters, Lake District waters vary, species present will differ, depths may change, and techniques need to be adapted, but they all have one factor in common. They are surrounded by some of the most beautiful and breathtaking scenery in the country. It is an environment into which anglers should be able to fit without being at all obtrusive.

Unfortunately there exists, as in all sports, a small undesirable element, whose main interest seems to give all other anglers a bad name, particularly by leaving litter. To these people let us say, your presence is not welcome. To the majority of true anglers, who can behave themselves, and enjoy the tranquility of the English Lake District, may we wish you the best of luck in the pursuit of your chosen species.

Geoff Parkinson   *James Holgate*

FOOTNOTE:

To the would be Lake District angler, we stress that even where the fishing is free you will still need to be in possession of a current North West Water Authority rod licence, available from most tackle shops in the area.

ACKNOWLEDGEMENTS

Appreciation is due to Joanna A. Langhorne for permission to reproduce the following fish illustrations: chub, dace and roach. Thanks also to the Freshwater Biological Association, Windermere and Dr. Peter Maitland for kindly allowing the use of illustrations from their 'Key to Freshwater Fishes of the British Isles'.

CLOSE SEASONS

LAKE DISTRICT (CUMBRIA)
North West Water Authority Rod Licence

Salmon — 1st November to 31st January inclusive; except in the River Eden and all waters connected with it, shall be from 15th October to 14th January inclusive.

Migratory Trout — 16th October to 30th April inclusive; except in the Rivers Annas, Bleng, Esk, Mite, Irt, Calder and Ehen and all connected waters, shall be from 1st November to 30th April.

Non-Migratory Trout — 1st October to 14th March. There is no close season for rainbow trout in enclosed waters, provided that during this period it shall be lawful to fish for eels.

Charr — 1st October to 14th March, except in the following waters:

Coniston — 1st November to 30th April

Windermere — 1st October to 30th April

provided that it shall be lawful from the 15th March to fish for charr with artificial lures from a moving boat.

Coarse Fish — 15th March to 15th June inclusive, in rivers and streams, and all named major Lakes (check licence). On all other waters there is no close season. However, some fishery owners do impose one.

LAKES and TARNS

ABBOT MOSS LAKE

Rainbow trout up to 4lbs have been stocked in this three acre fishery. To get there from Penrith, travel along the A6 to Carlisle, about seven miles along this road take the right hand turn off towards Lazonby. Half a mile down here you will see a sign outside a house advertising the sale of day tickets for the water, which is further along the road. Fishing is with fly only and starts on the 7th April. Telephone Calthwaite 282 for further information and advance bookings.

ALCOCK TARN

Located half way up Heron Pike to the east of Grasmere village. Formerly known as Buttercraggs Tarn, it was dammed and enlarged in the early 1900's by a Mr. Alcock who gave the water its present name as well as its stock of brown trout. The descendants of those fish can still be caught today; in general, they are not particularly large but they are plentiful and a pleasant change from the stew-fed stockies found in so many lowland waters. As tarns go, it is not a particularly difficult water to reach, the shortest route is up Greenhead Gill where a well trodden path will lead you to the water. The fishing is free.

ANGLE TARN (LANGDALE)

One of the most noticeable aspects of fishing in Cumbria is the vast number of small hill tarns, so many in fact that they often share a common name, very confusing for the visitor, when for example, he is advised that "Angle Tarn" is fishing well he will consult his map to find several waters of that name. Despite the rather hopeful connotations of such a name, many are little more than puddles but a couple at least might be worthy of your attentions. The first lies in Langdale Fell, a water of around six acres and with depths up to fifty feet. This is a really spectacular water to view but unfortunately the fishing doesn't match up to the scenery, only a few small trout manage to eke out an existence in its dark cold waters. The fishing is free.

ANGLE TARN (PATTERDALE)

A much bigger tarn of around fifteen acres and one which offers much better fishing prospects. Located just south of Patterdale it contains trout, perch, pike and eels. Can best be reached from Low Hartsop, a walk of around two miles from the A592 road to Ambleside. The water is around thirty feet deep and two islands in the water make for an interesting little tarn fishery. Enquire locally for permission to fish. Generally speaking, a better bet for the trout than the coarse angler.

BASSENTHWAITE LAKE

The most northerly of the big Cumbrian Lakes and, in many respects, one of the best. Amongst general coarse anglers it is best known for its stocks of perch, a species which can be caught in astonishing numbers at the right time of year. These fish seem to average between 8oz to 12oz and, at times, the margins of this four mile long water seem to be alive with this voracious but beautiful fish. The perch fishing seems to be best in the earliest part of the coarse fishing season, from June 16th onwards and they become less easy to tempt as the year progresses. Although most of the perch caught by anglers are small there are undoubtedly some very big fish also present. Fish up to 2½lbs to 3lbs are a definite proposition, the only reason they are not caught more often is mainly because so few anglers bother to set out to catch fish of this size.

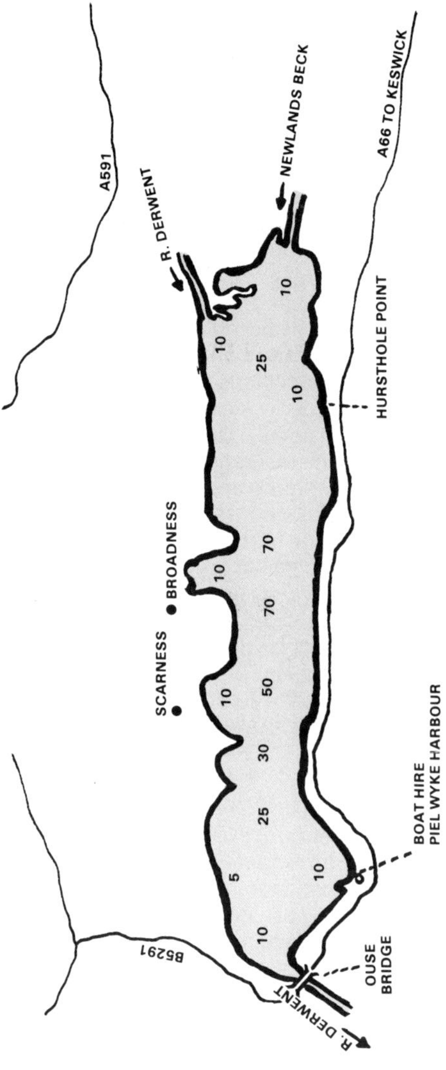

BASSENTHWAITE LAKE
(DEPTHS IN FEET)

A591

R. DERWENT

NEWLANDS BECK

A66 TO KESWICK

HURSTHOLE POINT

10

10

25

10

SCARNESS

BROADNESS

70

10

70

50

10

30

25

5

10

10

BOAT HIRE
PIEL WYKE HARBOUR

B5291

OUSE
BRIDGE

R. DERWENT

Eels are also very abundant in the lake during the warmer months; like the perch they range in size from small 'bootlaces' up to four pounders — and there are also persistent, if unconfirmed, reports of individual specimens double that size.

The pike fishing on this lake is well exploited these days and quite a few double figure fish are reported each season. The largest fish recorded from the lake was a 34lb specimen, and although that particular fish was caught many years ago there are still some twenty pounders taken from time to time. However, in the main, they average between seven to nine pounds.

For the game angler the situation is generally less hopeful; certainly, the lake is less renowned as a trout venue than many other lakes like Windermere, Ullswater and Coniston. The average size of the fish is small, fourteen ounces to a pound being above the norm. However, fish up to four pounds plus are present in the lake. Bassenthwaite is connected to nearby Derwentwater by the River Derwent which flows into the lake's southern end and out at the northern tip. As a result the lake has a run of salmon in the back end of the year. By most accounts the northern part of the lake around Ouse Bridge is a good starting point for both species.

One of the rarer species of freshwater fish is also present in the lake, this is the vendace, a small silvery fish which generally inhabits the deeper water around seventy foot. It is not encountered very often in this lake and you are more likely to see it washed up on the shore dead at spawning time than you are to catch one.

If you want to avoid the holiday crowds who descend on this beautiful lake in the summer months then a trek around to the lake's eastern shoreline is advisable. It's far less accessible than the western side, which runs parallel to the main A594, but the walk is often worthwhile, if only for the extra peace it affords. But do be careful, some parts of the eastern shore are strictly private.

One of the best ways of fishing the lake — especially in summer — is from a boat. Like most of the big lakes, with the exception of Windermere, no powered craft are allowed (except oar power). You can, if you wish, launch your own boat on the lake (provided you obtain a special permit to do so) from Piel Wyke in the north western corner (near the sailing club). Rowing boats can also now be hired from this same area.

All of Bassenthwaite is under the control of the Lake District Special Planning Board, and day permits can be obtained from the Warden on the bank.

BEACON TARN

Located high in the Blawith Fells, to the west of Lake Coniston, Beacon Tarn is another of those Lakeland waters which would be more suited to a party of sherpas! To reach the water, take the A5084 along the west bank of Coniston, at the southern end there is a small turn-off towards Water Yeat; this single track road ends at Greenholme Farm. From here the tarn is another quarter mile walk up hill along the public right of way towards Tarn Riggs.

The tarn, when reached, is a rather bleak and windblown venue with an average depth of around twenty feet dropping down to thirty feet in a couple of spots. In many respects a typical Lakeland hill tarn. The water is around eleven acres in extent and the two main species are trout and perch; charr are also said to be present along with a few pike. Very little is known about the water, certainly it is doubtful whether you will fish it in the presence of other anglers. The fishing is free.

BIGLAND COARSE FISHERY

A rather pleasant little lake overlooked by Bigland Hall. Its reed-lined waters hold healthy stocks of rudd, of which some large catches are made, there's also roach, tench, a few carp to about six pounds and of course, numerous perch and pike, the latter growing to double figures. A good all round coarse fishery. The water is controlled by Bigland Hall Sporting Estates and day permits can be obtained from the Estates Office which is at the entrance to the water and **must** be obtained in advance of fishing.

The water is situated close to the A590 Levens to Backbarrow road. To reach the water turn left at Backbarrow towards Brow Edge, the fishery and entry to the estate grounds is at the top of this steep hill.

BIGLAND TROUT FISHERY

A fairly recent addition to the stillwater trout fishing scene but one which has already found a place in the affections of most Cumbrian trout fishermen. The tarn is, in fact, man-made, the result of the blocking-off of a stream which produced the present five acre fishery. Like the previously mentioned coarse fishery this lake is also controlled by Bigland Hall Sporting Estates who keep the lake rigorously stocked at 100 fish per acre, and individual fish over eight pounds in weight are usually introduced along with the smaller fish. There is a four fish bag limit but if you fish barbless hooks you can carry on fishing all day, provided you return fish carefully to the water. For prices and further information telephone Newby Bridge 31361.

BLEA TARN (NEAR BOOT)

The people who first named these small Lakeland tarns seem to have shown a certain lack of imagination in their choice of names. For example, there are at least four "Blea Tarns" in the area ("blea" is actually the old Norse word for "blue") This particular one is situated a couple of miles west of the turn-off towards the small village of Boot. A short steep climb along the public right of way will bring you to the water. Brown trout and perch are present. The fishing is free.

BLEA TARN (LITTLE LANGDALE)

Yet another hill tarn of the same name. This one is often confused with its slightly bigger namesake further north at Watendlath. Located along the B5343 out of Elterwater village, the tarn is a short walk from Blea Tarn Farmhouse, Little Langdale, from where day permits can be obtained. The tarn itself is around forty acres in extent with a maximum depth of twenty-five feet. It is home to brown trout, perch and pike, none of which seem to grow very big.

BLEA TARN (NEAR WATENDLATH)

To reach this tarn, follow the same instructions as for Watendlath Tarn. When you have reached the small village of Watendlath, Blea Tarn is to be found a further mile up the small Blea Tarn Gill, which is the stream heading furthest east from the tarn — be careful to follow the correct stream. Less accessible than the others, Blea Tarn has a reputation for being a better trout water, although most trout caught will be the usual hill tarn sized five to eight ounces; there is also the chance of fish up to a pound or a little more. Take care though, much of the surrounding land can be a little boggy at times.

BLEA WATER

A tarn more noted for its astonishing depth than for its merits as a fish producer. It occupies an enormous bowl in the rugged mountains south of Haweswater — and the spectacular setting is matched by the waters own dimensions — with surface area of only forty acres the tarn descends to depths in excess of 200ft, a fact which must make this one of the deepest small waters in the country.

It's only a pity the tarn's resident trout don't live up to the monumental size of their home. Like most unremittingly deep waters, the trout, lacking the richer feeding of extensive shallows, are generally small and undernourished, but at least they are present in good numbers and very free biting. The fishery is free to anyone with the energy to clamber up with their tackle. To find the water you will need to follow the small stream (Bleawater Gill) which runs into the southern end of Haweswater, take the right hand stream when it divides in two, and the tarn is at the end of this stream.

BLELHAM TARN

In this instance, the word "tarn" might be a little misleading, implying as it does a rather rugged and remote water. Blelham, in fact, occupies a depression amidst rich farmland overlooking the western shoreline of Lake Windermere, close by the B5286 Ambleside to Hawkshead road. The tarn very much resembles a lowland lake, and its extensive surroundings of dense reed beds reinforces this impression. It is a rich water and very productive — if you can find a place to fish — those reed beds render about ninety percent of the banking inaccessible to the angler.

Trout, perch, pike and eels all grow well and if you should find a fishable spot you will probably not be disappointed by your results. This is a National Trust property and day permits are available from the Warden at the Low Wray Campsite about half a mile from the water.

BLENCARN LAKE

Set in the scenic Eden Valley and overlooked by Cross Fell six miles east of Penrith, this seven acre lake offers fly fishing for brown and rainbow trout which are stocked on a regular basis. There is a ten rod per day limit and both day (four fish limit) and evening (two fish) tickets can be obtained by getting in touch with J. K. Stamper, Blencarn Hall, Blencarn, Near Penrith, telephone Culgaith 284. All fish caught must be kept.

BORETREE TARN

Better described as an upland lake than a true tarn, this pleasant and moderately secluded water provides a gentle introduction to fishing the area's vast numbers of hill tarns, many of which would prove a lot more daunting to the newcomer. The lake has a flourishing stock of pike which seem to be getting smaller, a fish of over ten pounds would be the exception. The tarn also teems with small perch and in summer any remotely enticing bait dropped in to the water's margins will be eagerly taken by fish in the four to five inch range; there are some bigger samples present, up to two pounds, the first problem being how to avoid their small cousins. The tarn is not very productive of trout and few are caught.

The tarn has a maximum depth of forty feet and is around six acres in extent with one small island in the western corner. As the name hill tarn suggests, access to this water is via a fairly steep climb from the village of Finsthwaite near Newby Bridge in southern Lakeland. However, the climb is not as bad as many we could mention, it's just a question of travelling light. This water is now privately run and up-to-date information should be sought from Finsthwaite Estates.

BRAYTON POND

Very much off the beaten track as far as most tourists are concerned but Brayton Pond (only in the Lake District would an eight acre lake be called a pond!) has the distinction of being one of Cumbria's few carp fisheries. It is certainly one of the longest established and best known. It contains a fairly prolific stock of fully scaled common carp and hordes of oft-caught crucian carp. Most of the commons tend to be around six pounds, along with some lower to mid doubles. Not big by the standards of further south . . . but beggars can't be choosers.

The lake is located fifteen miles west of Carlisle, along the A596 at Brayton, near Aspatria. The water can be fished on a day ticket, which must be bought in advance of fishing from the house overlooking the lake. The water, as you might expect, is very heavily fished, particularly by matches at the weekends, therefore a mid-week visit is advisable. There is no night fishing. For further details about the pond contact Mr. R. H. Ward, Home Farm, Brayton, Aspatria, telephone Aspatria 20262.

BROTHERS WATER

Situated at Hartsop just near the foot of the Kirkstone Pass and connected to nearby Ullswater by the small Goldrill Beck, this forty acre lake is not generally as popular as its much bigger neighbour, with either tourists or anglers. Which is a pity, for whilst this little water cannot boast of the sheer volume of captures as Ullswater, the fish, particularly the trout, are plentiful.

This is another National Trust property and the fishing is free of charge for all species. The eastern bank is the most accessible and is but a short walk from the road side to the lake. Parts of the western shoreline are private and permission should be obtained from the riparian owners before fishing, although this would offer no real advantage as regulars on the lake maintain that the road side is just as productive.

The brown trout in the lake are plentiful and generally obtain a higher size than Ullswater, an average of fourteen

Brothers Water with the Kirkstone Pass in the background.

ounces being not uncommon. The perch are equally numerous but tend to be on the small side; very small eels can also be a nuisance when legering a bait in the warmer weather. Pike are also said to inhabit Brothers Water but reports of captures are few and hard to verify. The trout in particular seem to be at their most prolific around August but fly fishing will be badly hampered by large beds of surprisingly thick weed.

BURNMOOR TARN

Said to be the third biggest tarn in the district, in fact, it's as large as some of the smaller more famous lakes of the area (Brothers Water, Rydal, Elter Water for example). It's a free fishery containing brown trout, pike and perch and with its extensive areas of shallow water providing rich feeding in the northern end, they also grow fairly well. The snag is the tarn's location, a two mile walk from the village of Boot, so travel light to avoid heart failure. However, sport with numerous small trout, perch and surprisingly large pike often make the journey worthwhile.

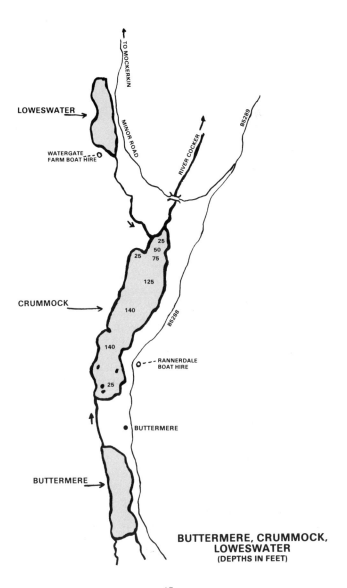

BUTTERMERE, CRUMMOCK, LOWESWATER
(DEPTHS IN FEET)

LOWESWATER

TO MOCKERKIN

MINOR ROAD

RIVER COCKER

B5289

WATERGATE
FARM BOAT HIRE

CRUMMOCK

B5288

RANNERDALE
BOAT HIRE

BUTTERMERE

BUTTERMERE

25
50
75
25
125
140
140
25

BUTTERMERE

There is a chain of three lakes in the far north western corner of the district, fairly hard to reach and little regarded by the majority of visiting anglers. Crummock is one, Loweswater another, and this lake is the third. Buttermere is one of the "smaller" of the English Lakes being around one and a half miles long and half a mile at its widest point with a maximum depth of ninety feet.

It provides fishing for brown trout, pike and perch. Charr are also present but seem to be quite rare and hardly worth the angler's serious attention. Like most of the big lakes, it fishes at its best in the summer months, the trout in particular find April and May to their liking and feed avidly during these months. The pike and perch show a similar preference for the warmer weather and June, July and August are the best months for both these species, neither of which are particularly heavily fished for in this lake.

The bay near Gatesgarth is always worth a try for most species and Burtness Wood in particular is a popular spot, but really this lake is very much an open and relatively little exploited book, one which would reward the attentions of the more adventurous coarse and game angler. Day permits are available from Gatesgarth Farm, Buttermere.

CLAY PITS FLY FISHERY

A ten acre lake situated between Cotehill and Cumwhinton two miles south east of Carlisle. Offers a well stocked fishery for rainbow and brown trout. The method is restricted to fly fishing and both day (four fish limit) and evening tickets (two fish limit) are available. For further details telephone Penrith 62542.

CLEABARROW TARN

Recently converted into a coarse fishery by Windermere, Ambleside & District A.A., this two acre lake now offers fishing for mirror carp, common carp and tench. The fish show every sign of growing well in the tarn's rich environment. It is situated close to the B5284, about five miles from Bowness, opposite Windermere Golf Course. The Association issue seven permits per day and these must be obtained before fishing from Smyth's Records, Ash Street, Bowness, telephone Windermere 3750. No night fishing, groundbaiting or keepnets are allowed.

CODALE TARN

To reach this tarn entails a two mile walk from the village of Easedale near Grasmere. The first tarn along the track is the larger Easedale Tarn, Codale is higher up and can be found by following the small stream which enters Easedale. When reached you will find a classic Lakeland hill tarn, a small circular hollow surrounded by mountains, with a stock of small brown trout which were originally brought up the steep track by persons long forgotten. The tarn is little fished these days, the majority of anglers wanting a bigger guaranteed stamp of fish than these small waters could provide, plus there's no car park. The fishing on the tarn is free.

Codale Tarn. A typically remote Lakeland hill tarn.

COGRA MOSS

This forty acre lake on Lamplugh Fell, four miles south west of Loweswater, offers fly fishing for the resident brown trout. Day permits are available from D. W. Lothian, Tackle Shop, 35 Main Street, Cockermouth, telephone 822006. A number of American brook trout are also sometimes stocked.

CONISTON WATER

Coniston is one of the areas richest waters, a fact which might well surprise anglers looking at the lake for the first time. Like most big Cumbrian Lakes, there's something about the clear water and craggy rock-strewn weedless banking that suggests a lack of enrichment, so vital to the growth of good fish stocks. Any angler coming to this conclusion, especially about Coniston, would be very much mistaken: like the other lakes, the apparently lifeless margins hide the true potential of its mysterious depths.

This five mile long water is home to brown trout, perch and pike, all of which I will come to later. But the lake's most important species is the charr, a fish which few visiting anglers will have encountered prior to visiting this area.

The fish, a landlocked relative of the salmon, generally inhabits the deeper water of the lake, which descends to 180ft in places. Rarely averaging more than fourteen ounces in weight but, with its sometimes crimson flanks, it is easily one of the most beautiful of our freshwater fishes.

As we have already mentioned, if you intend to go fishing for charr they are usually to be found in the deeper water over eighty feet or more. Boat fishing is particularly useful in this respect and certainly allows a great deal of ground to be covered in search of those elusive but vast charr shoals. Indeed, one of the most exciting ways of catching the fish is by trailing a small spinner from a light spinning rod. You will often pick up plenty of fish once you have found the depth at which they are feeding (which is not always on the lake's bottom).

Bank fishing, however, can also be extremely productive provided the choice of swim is even more carefully made, by seeking out places where the deeper water is within casting

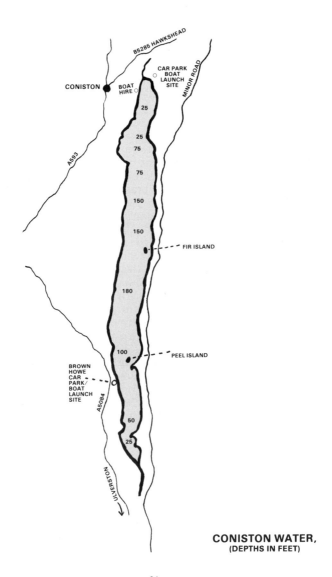

CONISTON WATER,
(DEPTHS IN FEET)

distance of the shore. Even when such spots have been found you will often find it necessary to make extremely long casts to find the shoal. Casts closer in produce more trout and perch. Snags, where rocky ledges suddenly plunge in to deeper water, can also be a big problem on this lake. The hot spots for the fish are well known by local anglers and regular visitors, perhaps a little too well known for the fishes good, and it is a common site to see clusters of green brollies around the better areas. Creditable attempts have been made by Coniston & Torver A.A. to reduce the pressure on the species and one of the most regularly used spawning grounds, along Brantwood Bank on the eastern shoreline, is now restricted, to stop the fish being over exploited when it is at its most vulnerable.

Brown trout are also abundant in the lake. Although not usually found in the numbers of Ullswater, or size of nearby Windermere, they are nonetheless well worth your attention. The north eastern shoreline seems to be one of the more productive areas, but all along the lake, in its shallow bays, free rising brown trout can be found in the warmer months, June is usually the most productive time. Like the charr, fishing from a boat, especially in the earliest part of the morning, will enable you to cover a lot of good ground.

Of the coarse fish, the perch are easily the most abundant, followed closely by eels in the warmer weather. Neither species seems to grow particularly big in this lake, a one pound specimen of either species seems to be the exception. The pike fishing on Coniston is quite good but the fish tend to be a little on the small side. The water authority culls them from time to time; even so, fish up to sixteen pounds can still be caught and a twenty pounder or two might also still be present.

The fishing on Coniston itself is free, provided you are in possession of a North West Water Authority Rod Permit. Do remember though, if you intend fishing for the charr you will need to buy the slightly more expensive trout permit, not the cheaper coarse licence. The season for charr fishing is at present from October 1st to April 30th, inclusive of those dates, and it should be remembered that maggots are banned as bait for this fish but brandlings or caddis grubs can be

Spinning for perch and trout on Coniston.

used. It should also be remembered that although the fishing is free, some parts of the banking are private, but these are usually well signposted. As for boats, these can be hired from the boat yard in Coniston Village but if you wish, it is possible to launch your own.

CRUMMOCK WATER

The middle lake of those three little regarded waters in the north west corner of the district, Crummock is by far the largest. With a length of two and a half miles, a quarter mile at its widest point and with a maximum depth of just over 140ft., this is no duck pond, and it is hard to see how a water of such dimensions can be so easily overlooked by the visiting angler.

The lake has brown trout, pike and perch as its three main species, charr are also present and are occasionally taken, but more often by anglers trolling deep lures intended for the bigger trout than as deliberate captures. Indeed, the lake is best known (as far as it is known at all) as a trout fishing venue. Not perhaps as productive as some of the area's other big lakes, but certainly well worth the game angler's attentions. Most of the fish average around half a pound but specimens of up to three pounds can also be encountered. May and June seem to be the two most productive months, at least as far as the fly fisher is concerned; the bait angler will find the trout to be free biting throughout the summer months.

The coarse fishing on the lake is far less well known or exploited. The perch, of course, make up the bulk of catches, but the few anglers who regularly fish for them say they tend to have a small average size with the occasional bigger fish of two pounds being reported from time to time. Eels can also be caught in the lake in the summer months.

The pike fishing is something of a mystery; few are reported from the lake and yet they are undoubtedly present, up to twenty pounds plus along with a lot of smaller fish, well worth a visit by the more adventurous pike angler.

Salmon and even a few sea trout also run into the lake from the River Cocker, which flows out of the lake's northern end. A few are sometimes taken, but mainly by anglers fishing for the brown trout.

For bank fishing for all species, with the exception of the charr, the water around or near the four small islands in the lake's southern corner can provide some good starting points for exploring the large expanse of water. At the other end of the lake, the woods which descend down to the water from Scale Hill are also a good bet, and the mouth of the River Cocker will also provide the best chance of hooking a salmon or sea trout. The charr will generally inhabit the deeper water, and Hause Point on the more accessible western side and Lings Crags on the more remote eastern bank will be worth a try for this species.

Day permits to fish the whole lake can be obtained from Rannerdale Farm which overlooks the water. Boats may also be hired at the same venue.

DERWENTWATER

Shallower and generally less popular than its near neighbour Bassenthwaite to which it is joined, Derwentwater is nonetheless worth more than a passing glance by the visiting angler. Like most of the big lakes, Derwentwater contains the usual mix of fish — pike, perch, trout — and they all seem to grow well in the rich environment which the lake provides.

Pike of over twenty pounds are certainly present in the three mile long water and writing in the late 1800's a Mr. John Watson in his book *The Lake District Fisheries* commented thus: "Pike abound in the lake and run to a large size, fish of twenty-nine pound and thirty-four pound having been obtained". However, the water does not seem to produce that calibre of fish today, but at least the angler will find plenty of fish in the seven pound to eight pound bracket to keep him occupied.

The lake also contains plenty of perch and these fish do seem to obtain a higher average size than many other lakeland waters. Fish of one and a half pounds can be caught from many parts of the lake and specimens of over three pounds have also been taken recently by anglers fishing the fly for trout.

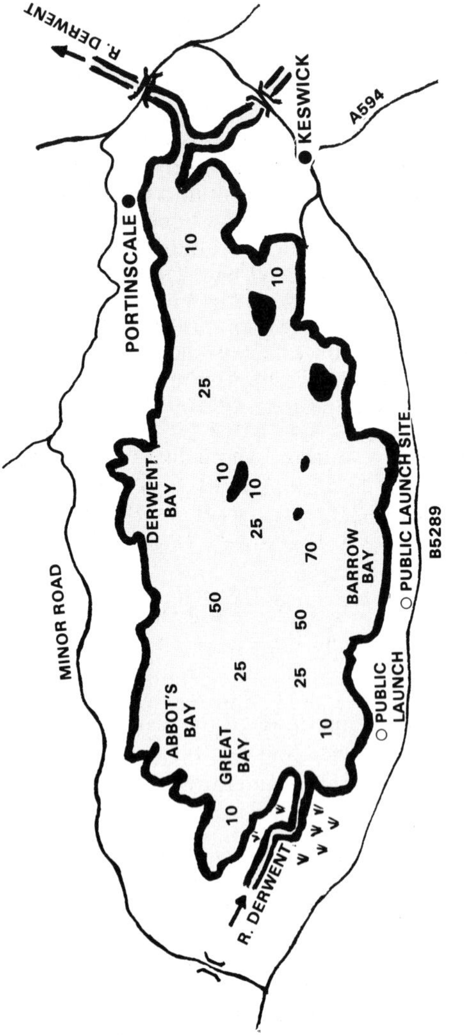

DERWENTWATER
(DEPTHS IN FEET)

R. DERWENT

KESWICK

A594

PORTINSCALE

MINOR ROAD

DERWENT BAY

ABBOT'S BAY

GREAT BAY

BARROW BAY

PUBLIC LAUNCH

PUBLIC LAUNCH SITE

B5289

R. DERWENT

10

10

25

10   10

25

50

25

25   50

70

10

10

But the lake should not be overlooked as a trout water either; although they don't grow very big, the brown trout of Derwentwater do at least have the distinction of providing good sport throughout the warmer months and well in to early autumn; most fish average around half a pound but fish up to three pounds can also be taken from time to time.

Indeed, generally speaking, the lake fishes best for all species in the summer months and this is possibly due to the shallower nature of the lake. There is, however, one big drawback, the lake is also a magnet for tourists at this time. This is not such a problem on other big waters in the area, where even in the height of the season it is usually possible to find some quiet little corner where tourists rarely go. This doesn't seem to be possible in Derwentwater, the WHOLE of the lake swarms with visitors in summer. Consequently, an early start is advisable, packing up for the day when you receive the first "caught any sharks yet? ha ha", from the day's first walker! If you must fish all day, then the western side will be your best bet. There is also a ferry service on the lake which plies a regular route; these steamers can create a terrific wash so take care not to leave any of your tackle too close to the waters edge.

There are plenty of rowing boats for hire at the Keswick end of the lake, and a boat will certainly help you to explore the many bays and inlets dotted around this interesting water.

The two large shallow bays at either end of the lake are certainly worth exploring in detail for all species. The rich feeding that the thick weed beds provide attracts all the lake's main species. The lake has four large islands and four smaller islets and the waters around these are also productive, especially of trout.

There is one more species we must consider before leaving Derwentwater and that is the vendace. Rarely exceeding nine inches in length this small deep water dwelling member of the white-fish family is said to inhabit the lake. However, the species capture has not been reliably reported for many years and is thought by many to be now extinct — a fate which also befell the species in Castle Loch, where changes in the water quality of the loch led to their eventual demise.

The water itself is controlled by Keswick A.A. and day tickets are available from Temple's Sports Shop, Station Street, Keswick.

DEVOKE WATER

The largest tarn in the Lake District and also somewhat remote. Situated in the south western part of the district, the fishing is controlled by Millom & District A.A. The fishing is for members of this club only, no day tickets are issued.

DRUNKEN DUCK TARN

What a marvellous name for a fishery! This small tarn is situated near the Drunken Duck Hotel, from where a limited number of day tickets are available for the water, which offers brown trout fishing with methods limited to fly fishing only. The hotel and water are to be found near the B5286 road to the west of Ambleside.

EASEDALE TARN

Twenty-five acres in extent, this popular tourist spot lies just three miles from the village of Grasmere (up hill of course!). The location of the tarn is well signposted and the well-trodden nature of the wide track will give some indication of the water's popularity, with walkers not anglers. The tarn is considerably less daunting than many in the area and we would recommend a place like this for your first introduction to the charms of fishing these high level waters — lacking, as it does, the almost lunar-like surroundings of some of the really remote lakeland waters.

There is a healthy stock of native brown trout to be caught which can be very obliging and are particularly partial to a float-fished worm, as are the perch which also inhabit the tarn's depths. Eels also find their way into the tarn in surprising numbers. The tarn is around sixty feet in depth at certain points but is considerably shallower around the large boulder which is a distinctive feature. The fishing on the tarn is free.

EEL TARN

One of a cluster of small waters around the village of Boot, to the south of Wastwater. The fishing is free for small brown trout, it seems to be fished about once every ten years! Don't be fooled by the name, it is doubtful whether the tarn actually contains any eels; the name is probably a corruption of another word of Norse origins. Further to the east and a slightly higher climb is Stoney Tarn where the fishing is again free.

ELLISCALES PONDS

Near to the A595 between Dalton and Askham-in-Furness, this group of flooded mine shafts provides fairly good coarse fishing. Tench, perch, rudd and a few bream are present in each of the pits in varying quantities. The three biggest are Figure Eight, Banana and Elliscales itself. Generally speaking, the perch are the most numerous species in all the pits, with the rudd also growing quite big, especially in Figure Eight Pond. They are all very, very deep and care should be taken when fishing them as they go from a few inches to what seems like a few hundred feet in one short step from the bank. As such we wouldn't personally advise any unaccompanied youngsters to fish them. Day permits are available from Mr. Wilf Rigg, Elliscales Farm, Dalton-in-Furness, which is the farm by the road side. Night fishing is allowed with prior permission.

ELTER WATER

Lying between Ambleside in the east and Grasmere further north this most shallow of the bigger lakes is better known as a tourist attraction than an angling venue. It is certainly a pleasant little water to look at, with its wooded banking and overlooked by the distant mountains of the Langdale Pikes.

The lake contains pike, perch and a few trout, very little fished, which either means it is a water of untapped potential or it's just no good! Enquire locally for permission to fish. But don't forget that Loughrigg Tarn is just half a mile away and might be a better prospect for the visiting angler with only a little time to spare.

A tench from Elliscales Ponds for angler David Standing.

ENNERDALE LAKE

Enner where? might well be the response when this least exploited (what an awful word) of the English Lakes is mentioned. It is, in truth, very much off the beaten track, and serviced by a single minor road from Cleator Moor which reaches just the lake's western tip. As far as the angler is concerned, this is all to the good, and Ennerdale is one of the best places to go for relatively aggravation-free fishing.

The lake provides good fishing for both brown trout and charr, surprisingly there are no perch or pike in the water. July and September seem to be the best times for the trout, which are very numerous if somewhat small, a fish over a pound is a real specimen. The charr are less commonly caught but this might be because they are less exploited (that awful word again!) than in most other lakes. Like other waters they are most often encountered in the deeper water, especially where the lake shelves steeply, but in Ennerdale they are also sometimes taken by anglers fishing wet flies intended for the trout. The average size of the charr is on the small side, around half a pound or less.

Generally speaking, the lake's shallower northern end is the best bet for the trout. Bowness Knott on the north bank and the hopefully named bay around Angler's Crag provide good starting points for exploring the lake.

Day permits can be obtained from Hall's Hardware Shop, South Street, Egremont. A few boats are also available for hire, enquire at the Angler's Inn close to the water.

ESTHWAITE WATER

Lying amidst the gentler rolling hills of southern Lakeland, beautiful Esthwaite Water is the only big Cumbrian Lake holding stocks of rainbow trout and, in many respects, this one and a half mile long fishery is the ideal recipient for these relative newcomers to the Lakeland angling scene.

Controlled and stocked by the Hawkshead Trout Farm the lake is fast becoming a favourite amongst the area's many angling visitors. It's an any-method fishery and because it is stocked with non-breeding rainbows, it is open all year round. The trout seem to have adapted well to their new home and although most fish stocked into the water by the farm have been in the three-quarter pound class for the last few years, fish in the eight to nine pound bracket have occasionally been caught.

Although bank fishing is popular and indeed much of the banking is readily accessible from the roads which skirt the lake, many anglers prefer to hire a rowing boat (powered craft are forbidden). These can be obtained from the farm which is located along the lake's south western shore and is well signposted. However, only a few boats are available and it is advisable to book one in advance.

The fishery is truly an all-year-round water and fishes well even in December but if there is a really heavy frost the fish will be dour and unresponsive. For further details contact The Hawkshead Trout Farm, Foldgate, Hawkshead, telephone 541.

GHYLL HEAD RESERVOIR

A newly opened water of around eleven acres under the control of Windermere and District A.A. The club stocks the water with rainbow trout and there is also a good stock of wild brownies averaging a pound in weight. For day permit details see the entry under Moss Eccles Tarn.

GOATS WATER

Words like "craggy" and "rugged" will possibly spring to mind when the angler first sets his or her eyes on remote Goats Water. This is Lakeland tarn fishing at its most forbidding. The tarn lies at the foot of Dow Crag which tumbles down to meet its western shoreline and is overlooked by Coniston Old Man towards the east. To reach the water will entail a walk of around three and a half miles from the village of Coniston; it should be quite easy to locate, just follow all those people wearing bright orange Kagools and earnest expressions!

Whether the hour and a half walk is considered worthwhile will depend, to a large extent, on your expectations. If you are looking for a catch of small brown trout in the four to eight ounce range with the chance of catching one of the tarn's equally diminutive charr then this is the water for you; if you are looking for something larger or more productive don't make the effort. The fishing is free.

GRASMERE

Located directly alongside the main A591 Keswick/Ambleside road, which skirts the lake's eastern shoreline. As far as Lakeland waters go, it is small, around one mile in length and with a maximum depth of between fifty or sixty feet. Despite its size, with the exception of Windermere, this little lake is possibly the one most associated in the minds of the general public with "The Lakes". It's easy to reach and one of the more popular lakeland walks skirts around its shores, and it shows. The place is crawling with tourists practically the year round but, if you choose the times with care, it is still possible to catch fish.

The lake contains perch, pike and brown trout and these days it is better known for the two former species than the latter. Perch, as usual, are by far the most numerous species in the lake and can be caught from most parts of the shoreline. Spinning or worm fishing are both very effective but a small minnow livebait will often sort out the bigger fish of a pound or more. The pike of Grasmere tend to average around five pounds but a few twenty pounders are also caught from time to time.

A good way to fish the lake is by boat and these can be hired from the Grasmere village end of the lake or, if you wish, it is also possible to launch your own boat as there is a launch site located in the same area.

Grasmere is actually not as convenient to reach as it first appears, just two small (two car) lay-bys along the A591 are all the parking facilities you will find close to the lake, so it's a good idea to get there early to grab one of the few places. The lake is now under the control of Windermere and Ambleside A.A. Day permits are widely issued, the two nearest sellers being Broadgates Newsagents, Grasmere and most Tourist Information Centres also sell the club's permits.

GREENDALE TARN

One of three small and little fished hill tarns located to the north of Wastwater, the other two being Low and Scoat Tarns. All three involve a lot of walking to reach them, and all offer free fishing for small brown trout.

GREEN HOWS TARN

Situated in a quiet and private woodland area, two and a half miles north of Newby Bridge, Green Hows Tarn offers the trout fisherman the chance of catching reasonably-sized brown and rainbow trout. Day tickets for this two and a half acre water are available from the house opposite the fishery, which is visible from the road. There is a three fish limit and the season starts on the 1st April. Fly only. To get there from Newby Bridge, take the road to Hawkshead, at Low Graythwaite turn left and the water can be seen on the left, half way up the hill.

GRISEDALE TARN

Another high level fishery with an altitude above sea level of 1,768ft. Is said to contain bigger trout than the average hill tarn, by "big" we mean fish in the eight to twelve ounce bracket. It is situated two miles from the south eastern corner of Thirlmere. To find it, park on the A591 at High Broadrayne and follow the public right-of-way up the Grisedale Hause, the tarn is along this path. The water is fairly deep in places with a maximum depth of just over one hundred feet.

HALL MORE FLY FISHERY

As the name suggests, this is a fly only water situated at Hale near Milnthorpe. Rainbow trout are regularly stocked into this three acre fishery. Half and full day tickets are available. For directions and to book tickets in advance telephone Milnthorpe 2375.

HARROP TARN

A small water south west of Thirlmere, rather shallow, weedy and very hard to fish. Provides free fishing for brown trout and perch.

HAWESWATER

Not strictly speaking a lake, but a reservoir, created in the 1940's when a 120ft dam was constructed at the head of the valley, thus enlarging the original small Haweswater into the four mile long "lake" we know today.

With a maximum depth of 190ft at the dam end, Haweswater is one of the few lakes in the country containing the schelly, a deep-water dwelling species of whitefish also found in Ullswater and Red Tarn. In fact, Haweswater has most recently hit the headlines when a real specimen of this species was landed, weighing 2lb 1½oz; the fish easily beat the existing record — a 1lb 10oz fish caught from Ullswater.

Although this is not, strictly speaking, a "how to catch them" type of book, a few pointers about the habits of this rare fish would not come amiss. As has already been mentioned the fish seems to prefer the deeper waters over eighty feet, and if you are looking for a good swim then one where these kind of depths are within casting range should be sought. At one time it was thought the schelly would not take any kind of bait which the angler could practically present, yet more recent evidence shows that their capture on anglers' baits need not be a chance in a million. The fish has a definite preference for small worms presented on light leger tackle and care should be taken to provide the absolute minimum resistance to a taking fish, using little weight and the most sensitive bite indication the angler can devise. Naturally at the kind of depths we are considering, float fishing would generally be impractical. The schelly has also been taken on the fly on several occasions, although whether this would be practical in most circumstances is hard to say.

There are also some fairly abundant stocks of that other deep water fish in the reservoir, the charr, but they are generally a little on the small side — a fish of over half a pound would be the exception. With other more productive venues like Windermere and Coniston nearby, the Haweswater charr shoals remain relatively untouched.

But the lake is still best known as a productive venue for the brown trout angler. The fish are very prolific and rise well to a fly, particularly around June and July. Unfortunately, the lake doesn't have a reputation for producing big fish, although it has to be said that it is not as extensively fished as some of the better known Lakeland trout waters.

Day tickets are available from either the Haweswater Hotel, situated half way along the water's side or from Bampton Post Office, Bampton.

HIGH DAM

Situated to the south west of Lake Windermere, between the village of Finsthwaite and Low Stott Park. The water is around ten acres in extent and has the distinction of being one of the few Lakeland tarns with a thriving population of rudd. Brown trout and perch are also present in good numbers. It is certainly a very pleasant water to fish and the shoals of resident rudd can be very obliging with the bonus of the occasional trout.

The area round the lake is a popular tourist area (what area in the Lakes isn't these days?) and its location is well signposted with a car park at the foot of the uphill path leading to the tarn. From there follow the well-worn track through the woods; you will first come upon a small water of less than half an acre with a dam rising up at the far end behind which the waters of the main tarn are to be found. The fishing is free.

HOLEHIRD TARN

"Tarn" is really a rather loose description to apply to this pleasantly landscaped pool. It does, however, contain a good stock of coarse fish, with tench, chub, roach and perch

*Be prepared for a windy day's fishing in the Lakes . . .
at **any** time of the year!!*

being the species most likely to be encountered by the visiting angler. There is also a modest head of carp up to fifteen pounds though these fish have a reputation for being difficult to catch.

To find this water, take the A592 out of Windermere towards Patterdale. A short distance along this road you will see on your right a large tree-lined drive signposted "Holehird Cheshire Home". Go up the drive and a short distance from the entrance there is a car park. The lake is a short walk from here. Day permits are available from the garden's ground staff. DO NOT enquire about the fishing at the main house or the entrance lodge. When visiting the water you will notice a number of yellow posts dotted around the lake and the angler is restricted to fishing in swims marked thus. Can be a bit frustrating, hope the idea doesn't catch on. Permits are limited to eight per day.

KENTMERE TARN

A former natural tarn now converted into a reservoir. It is controlled by Staveley Angling Association who stock with brown and rainbow trout. Membership of the Association is restricted to local anglers. Further enquiries to Mr. D. Taylor, 18 Raws Garth, Staveley, Kendal, LA8 9QH.

KILLINGTON RESERVOIR

Many anglers will have caught sight of this large expanse of water from the M6 motorway, overlooked as it is by the Killington Service Station. The water in question is, in fact, a "top up" reservoir for the Lancaster Canal. It is high, open and windswept and is a popular venue for windsurfers but is still worth looking at for its undoubted angling potential.

It is ostensibly run as a trout water but seems to attract the coarse fisherman more these days. There are some good stocks of pike in the water, fish of over twenty pounds have been caught but be pleased with anything into double figures. Whatever size you catch, they are certainly amongst some of the most strikingly marked examples of this species you will ever encounter. The perch are also numerous and can be caught in abundance around most of the lake's margins in the summer months. They are mostly caught in the half pound weight range but bigger specimens up to two pounds are also there. A few roach, eels and the odd (very odd) tench are also in the water but none seem to exist in any great numbers. Certainly not enough to make a special journey worthwhile.

Depths in the reservoir vary between fifteen to twenty feet with the shallower weedy bays being a good bet in the summer. The area around the dam wall is out of bounds to anglers.

The most direct route to the water is on the A684 from Kendal towards Sedbergh; along this road you will pass over the M6 motorway bridge at Junction 37 and the road to Killington is a few hundred yards further on the right. Kent Angling Association have the fishing rights to this water. Day tickets can be obtained from the Reservoir Keeper, who is located at the large farm house near the dam, where all the boats are moored. Maggots are not allowed as bait.

LEVERS WATER

Situated high in the Coniston Fells, two miles north west of Coniston village and, in common with a surprising number of Lakeland waters, has been enlarged at some time in the distant past by the addition of a dam. The resulting larger sheet of water is well supplied with brown trout which are abundant if not exactly big, averaging around six to eight ounces. The water is quite deep with a maximum of around 100ft in a couple of places. To find the water you will need to walk some distance from Coniston along an old quarry track; it's a popular route for walkers, and the tarn's location will be well known to most of them. The fishing is free.

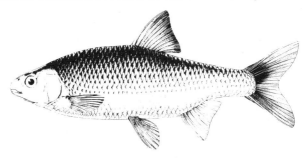

Roach

LOUGHRIGG TARN

A pleasant change this particular tarn, instead of a gruelling trek up some remote mountain, Loughrigg can be reached after a short walk **downhill.** I bet you were beginning to think there was no such water in the whole area! The tarn can best be viewed from the minor road which leads from Skelwith Bridge towards Little Loughrigg. It is quite large, almost the same size as nearby Elter Water.

The tarn holds a large head of roach and produces some good catches of this unusual Lakeland species — mainly in the summer. There's also a good stock of perch and pike up to around fifteen pounds. There are some trout in the water and although the tarn was once renowned as a venue for this species, they seem to have gone into something of a decline. Maximum depths are around thirty feet and its pleasant wooded and reed-lined banking makes for one of the "nicer" tarns in the area.

The water itself and the land surrounding it are the property of the National Trust. Day permits are available from Tarn Foot Farm which overlooks the water. The farmer will also allow anglers to park their cars in the farm yard, just a short walk away.

LOWESWATER

Crummock, Buttermere and Loweswater, those three "other" lakes tucked away in a remote north western corner of the district can all offer the visiting angler good sport at the right time of year and it's really hard to choose which is best, but Loweswater is certainly the least daunting. The lake is only about one and a half miles in length, much smaller than nearby Crummock; it is also shallower, with a maximum depth of only fifty feet and the surrounding woodland extending to the lake shore certainly does give a justifiable impression of richness not so readily apparent at some other lakes.

To a certain extent, this impression proves to be correct. Certainly, the resident brown trout show a comparatively good growth rate and fish of over a pound to a pound and a half are there for the catching along with the smaller fish. The lake is a good bet for the fly fisher, particularly in June and early July when the trout seem to be at their most active on or near the surface.

In common with most Lakeland waters, the perch are prolific and can be caught in good numbers from most parts of the lake, fish of three pounds plus have been caught but naturally most average about half a pound or slightly less. Pike over twenty pounds are undoubtedly present in the lake but possibly due to the abundant food stocks they are not so inclined to take baits.

The entire north eastern shoreline is easily accessible and runs within a few yards of the B5289. The far bank is considerably less accessible but the walk to Home Wood on that side is often worthwhile as the wooded slopes are a noted hot spot for most species — park your car in the park at the southern end of the lake and prepare yourself for a long foot slog. The best way to reach Loweswater is from the A5086 from Cockermouth turning towards the lake at Mockerkin.

Permits to fish are available from the Scale Hill Hotel, Loweswater, telephone Lorton 232. Rowing boats can also be hired from the same venue, useful if you want to explore that far bank.

MEADLY RESERVOIR

Situated some twelve miles from the town of Cleator Moor in west Cumbria, this twenty acre reservoir can be fished with a day ticket, available from the Post Office, Wath Brow, near Cleator Moor, telephone 801337. The water is controlled by Wath Brow and Ennerdale A.A. and is open from the 20th March to the 31st October. Brown trout is the predominant species. Permits must be obtained before fishing.

MOCKERKIN TARN

Located alongside the A5086 to Cockermouth, the tarn can, in fact, be seen from the lay-by just after the turn-off towards Loweswater. It is a pleasant little water, rather shallow, with a maximum depth of ten feet and, combined with the large expanses of water lilies, is very suggestive of coarse fish and indeed this is what the water is best known for. Containing pike, perch and more recently a good head of carp, this Tarn fishery is now controlled by Workington A.A. who at this present time do not issue day tickets.

MOSS ECCLES TARN

This nine and a half acre water is controlled by Windermere, Ambleside and District A.A. Located just to the east of Esthwaite Water, the tarn offers brown trout fishing with methods restricted to fly only. There is a two fish bag limit. Day permits are available and can be bought from most Tourist Information Centres in the area. Nearby High Arnside Tarn, Rydal Water and Grasmere can be fished on the same permit. Season permits are also available.

NEW MILLS TROUT FISHERY

A small water of only one acre, which offers fly fishing for rainbow trout up to four pounds in weight. To find the water, travel along the A69 out of Carlisle turning right at Brampton village. The water is one mile further along this road and signposts will direct you to the water side. There is a five fish bag limit and the water is open all year round, although in summer it is advisable to book in advance, especially at weekends. For further details contact New Mills Trout Fishery, New Mills, Brampton, telephone 2384.

ORMSGILL LOWER RESERVOIR

Right in the town of Barrow, this large and relatively unlovely reservoir is under the control of the Furness Fishing Association. The water contains trout, tench and carp. Unfortunately, no day permits are issued and membership of the Association is limited to anglers living within the South Lakeland area. For membership you would be advised to ask at one of the local tackle shops, Hannay's, 50 Crellin Street, Barrow, telephone 22571 is your best bet.

OVER WATER

Said to be the fourth largest tarn in the Lake District, although this is a bit of a cheat, as the water has been artificially enlarged by the construction of a dam to supply nearby Wigton. It is certainly a large expanse of water and can be seen on even the most rudimentary maps lying just to the north east of Bassenthwaite.

The water offers good fishing for rainbow trout and is in fact under the control of the Lake District Trout Farm. At the present time the ownership, particularly with regard permission to fish, is a little uncertain, so ask locally for updated information.

RED TARN

Nestling in the shadow of 3,118ft Helvellyn and itself having an altitude of over 2,000ft, Red Tarn is only for those anglers with determination and stamina. Indeed, few bother to make the effort. The tarn offers fishing for small brown trout — and spectacular scenery. Schelly, those deep water denizens of Ullswater and Haweswater, are also said to lurk in depths over sixty feet but few are ever encountered and their existence possibly owes more to legend than fact.

The fishing is free, the only expenditure will be energy. The easiest ascent is from Thirlspot on the western side of Helvellyn, but take care, this mountain range has the reputation of hosting more accidents on its craggy slopes than anywhere else in Cumbria.

ROAN HEAD FISHERIES COMPLEX

This group of old flooded mine workings has a reputation for providing some of the best coarse fishing in the south Lakeland area. There are six waters in all, from massive twenty-five acre Rita Pond to the smaller waters of Florence, Low, High Ponds, Moorfoot and Burnhole. They all have one common factor in being very, very deep.

Carp over twenty pounds, pike, tench, roach, perch, bream and eels are all present in good numbers. All the waters are clustered together on one site just north west of the town of Dalton-in-Furness. Furness Fishing Association hold the fishing rights to all six ponds. For permit details see Ormsgill Lower Reservoir.

RYDAL WATER

Just three-quarters of a mile long and quarter of a mile wide Rydal is one of the smallest of the English Lakes. It is connected to nearby Grasmere by the River Rothay which flows through the lake and onwards to Windermere a few miles further south. Small it may be, but this beautiful little lake is one of the areas most popular tourist spots and this fact more than anything can spoil the lake for the visiting angler. However, it is possible to fish the water in relative tranquility and local angler Chris Sodo suggests: "Anyone fishing Rydal will find the fishing a lot more peaceful on the western road bank or towards the northern end away from the popular western footpath. The west bank is constantly tramped by walkers and tourists. Rubber dinghys, dogs chasing sticks, swimmers and stone throwing kids are a great disturbance and you get a bit cheesed off when the six hundredth passerby asks you what you've caught!"

The entire water is under the control of Windermere, Ambleside and District A.A. who issue permits from a large number of sources including Broadgates Newsagents, Grasmere, and most local Tourist Information Offices. There are trout, perch and pike in the lake, the two latter species being the more prolific.

The lake's most immediately striking feature is the large Heron Island which practically cuts the water in two, and certainly the underwater contours of each section seem to be highly distinctive. The top half, towards the incoming River Rothay, is shallower, with depths of between five to eight feet. The lake below the island shows a much greater variation. As a result, it is well worth taking the trouble to plumb the depths carefully before choosing where to fish.

Rydal is certainly well served with car parks with one close to the western end just off the A591. There is another smaller park at the other end which can be found by crossing the small "rustic" bridge over the outgoing River Rothay; this park is the best bet if you intend to fish the western bank. A good water for a short very early morning fishing session before the crowds arrive for the day. If you have time, try throwing a small plug or spinner around the incoming River Rothay, just before it enters the lake; a surprisingly 'pikey' looking stretch of water, deep and fairly overgrown, it almost shouts of the species.

SEATHWAITE TARN

Following Tarn Beck from Seathwaite, the walk along this little valley will lead directly to the tarn. It is quite a rugged piece of water with a maximum depth of about eighty-five feet, which for a tarn, is large. There's trout a plenty although, as is often the case with these high level fisheries, they tend to be a little small, but extremely obliging. Controlled by the Furness Fishing Association, for ticket details see Ormsgill Lower Reservoir.

SKELSMERGH TARN

To reach this water, take the A6 north out of Kendal and the tarn is two and a half miles along this road down a small turn-off to the right. A short walk to a copse of trees will bring you to the water. It is really only a small pond of around one acre which contains masses of stunted roach and rudd. The fishing is free, but take care, the banking surrounding most of the lake is extremely boggy.

TALKIN TARN

Pike and perch are present in this small lake some eight miles east of Carlisle, near the town of Brampton. The fishing is free, although you will have to seek permission for access to the water from the riparian owners.

THIRLMERE

The large dam at this "lake's" northern end betrays the real purpose of this three and a half mile long sheet of water. Thirlmere is a large reservoir, built in the 1930's to supply the needs of the industrial north. But that description doesn't really do the water justice, the lake and surrounding landscape are actually one of the areas more popular "views", the subject of a thousand bad polaroids. At one time a nice view would have been all that the majority of anglers ever got — Thirlmere used to be very much off-limits to the general public — but this is changing as the North West Water Authority opens up the water to leisure activities.

The reservoir is now run as a free fishery. So far, results indicate that the water has not got the potential of some other Lakeland waters, either as a coarse or game venue, but that might be because so few anglers seem to be taking the trouble to give this new water a try. Even so, those anglers who are fishing the water suggest that the trout are numerous and seem to be well fed, the pike and perch too are turning up in good numbers, mainly in summer. Winter visitors report poor to non-existent catches of all species.

The lake is easily accessible with a car park at the northern end, where the minor road of the western side crosses the dam; another car park exists at the southern end on the same side. The lake has a maximum depth of 150ft, although shallower depths will generally be found, especially in the southern end.

Fishing on the reservoir is free, although anglers must be in possession of the correct NWWA Rod Licence, i.e. a trout one to fish for trout and a coarse one for the pike and perch; the chances are that you will be checked for the relevant permits on this lake. Methods are restricted however; fly fishing for the trout; sea fish dead baits only for the pike and spinning for the perch.

THORNSHIP HOUSE LAKE

Situated two miles from Shap along the A6, this one acre lake offers fly fishing for rainbow and brown trout. The water is open all year round. There is a three fish bag limit. For further details contact Alan Owen, telephone Shap 366.

THURSTONFIELD LOUGH

Why a "Lough" should be situated in Cumbria is a mystery to us. There is no mystery about the fishing though, brown, rainbow and American brook trout are regularly stocked into this forty acre water. It is situated four miles to the west of Carlisle, very close to the B5307 at Kirkbampton. It is a popular water, well stocked and run very much as a commercial venture. Advance booking is advisable, to do so contact M. H. Stordy, Lough House, Thurstonfield, telephone Burgh-by-Sands 431.

T'OVER TARN

Also known as "Blind Tarn". Little visited and rarely fished, this small water occupies a scooped-out hollow directly beneath the summit of Buck Pike in the fells west of Coniston Lake. Apart from the usual small brown trout, the tarn's only other claim to fame is the stock of small charr it contains. The fishing is free.

ULLSWATER

Seven miles in length, three quarters of a mile at its widest point and with a maximum depth of 200ft, even the bare statistics of Ullswater cannot fail to impress the visiting

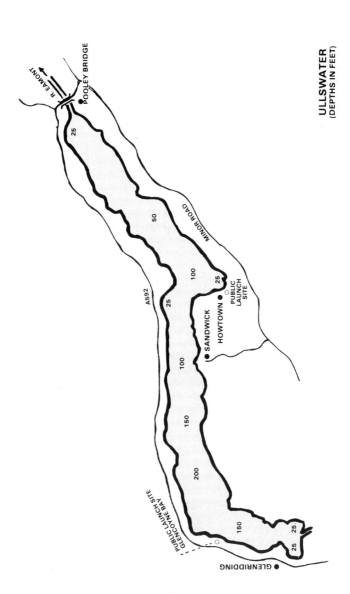

ULLSWATER
(DEPTHS IN FEET)

POOLEY BRIDGE

R. EAMONT

25

50

MINOR ROAD

100

25

A592

25

PUBLIC
LAUNCH
SITE

SANDWICK

HOWTOWN

100

150

200

PUBLIC LAUNCH SITE
GLENCOYNE BAY

150

25

25

25

GLENRIDDING

angler. One of Cumbria's most majestic lakes, set against the craggy backdrop of 2000ft Place Fell, it typifies, possibly more than any other lake, the almost harsh beauty of the area.

To the angler, Ullswater is perhaps best known these days for its trout fishing. In fact, the species is present in absolutely staggering numbers . . . and now the bad news, plentiful they may be, but they don't run to any great size —six to eight ounces would be a good average. However, they do make up for this deficiency by being very obliging . . . and tasty.

Although it is possible to drop on to a shoal of trout at any point around the lake's shoreline, places like the bay at Howtown on the less frequented eastern bank and the wide bay at Sandwick are both useful starting points. The more accessible shallows at the Pooley Bridge end of the lake can also be worth a try.

That other prolific Lakeland species, the perch, also finds the water very much to its liking. Summer especially sees the fish being caught in good numbers and they seem to be particularly numerous at the southern corner of Glenridding.

As we have already mentioned, this is one of the deeper lakes and depths of over 100ft can be found within casting distance of some parts of the shoreline. For most of the species in the lake, such depths will not be found to be the most productive; the shallower bays already mentioned and others around the lake should be sought.

There is one species lurking in those mysterious depths which you might just come across and that's the schelly. Also known as the skelly, gwyniad or even "freshwater herring", it is a small member of the salmon family and in Cumbria is only present in Haweswater and allegedly Red Tarn. They do look rather like herrings but they have the small adipose fin, so typical of a member of the salmon family. It is certainly one of the country's rarest fish and even in Ullswater its capture is an infrequent event. However, some anglers deliberately setting their stall out for the species have been rewarded with modest catches, ranging in size from a

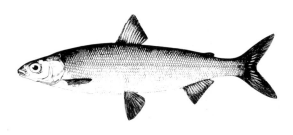

Schelly

few ounces up to a pound. The western side seems to be the most productive area for this fish.

That other deep water dwelling species, the charr, is also supposed to be present in the lake's depths, but few recent reports of the fish being caught exist and many pundits suggest that the species, if not already extinct, is on the verge of disappearing from this lake.

Another mystery concerns the pike — most accounts would suggest that the species does not exist at all in this lake — we're not so sure. Reports of anglers being broken by large fish whilst spinning with light tackle for perch with light lines and sightings made by scuba divers suggest that the species is present, but perhaps only in isolated pockets around the lake and not generally in numbers that would make fishing for them worthwhile.

There is also an early autumn run of salmon into the lake from the River Eamont which flows out of the lake's northern tip.

A boat is a good way of exploring the full potential of this lake, especially in the crowded holiday season and these can be hired from the boat yards at either Glenridding in the south of the lake or Pooley Bridge up in the northern tip. The fishing on the lake is free provided you have the relevant North West Water Authority Rod Licence. Most of the lake's north western shoreline is easily accessible as the A592 runs directly along its entire length, although parking in some places can be a bit of a problem; there is also a minor road along much of the other bank.

ULVERSTON CANAL

One of the most unusual angling venues in the area, the only canal in the whole of Cumbria. Stretching for just one and a quarter miles at Ulverston in the south of the county it is also one of the more consistent coarse fisheries.

It contains roach, bream, tench, a few carp, pike, perch, eels and chub. The roach and bream are the two most common species caught — not generally very big specimens but some large nets are taken. There is also plenty of tench up to around two and a half pounds with a few bigger fish up to four pounds.

The canal is extremely accessible being located directly behind the Canal Tavern on the A590 into Ulverston. Just turn down the side of this pub and there's the canal. Good news for real lazy bones, there is a single track road running along the entire length of the canal — in theory you can fish from your car!

It's quite wide for a canal, about double the width of the more traditional type, and there are also three large basins dotted along its short length; it is also completely boat free. The water is of a fairly even depth, between eight and nine feet, although it does shallow up considerably near the small, low (not the high one) railway bridge, halfway along the canal.

The canal is venue to many matches during the summer and especially at weekends. They are usually booked in advance and a notice telling anglers which pegs are booked should be posted at the start of the road leading on to the canal, worth checking before starting to fish or you might get moved from your chosen swim to make way for the competitors. Day tickets are available on the bank and the bailiff will come round to collect your money whilst you are fishing.

URSWICK TARN

Situated two and a half miles from Ulverston, in the village of Great Urswick, this small tarn is best known for the large number of small bream it contains, fish which can be caught in good numbers in most reasonable weather conditions. Tench up to about two and a half pounds can also be expected, but not in the same numbers as the prolific bream. Roach, perch, eels and roach/bream hybrids are also present in lesser quantities.

Permits are available from the Derby Arms in Urswick Village, or from the bailiff on the bank. Not all of the tarn is fishable, however, as much of the surrounding land is private; access is generally limited to a specially constructed wooden platform around one section of the lake. A few boats are sometimes available for hire, enquiries should be made at the boat house.

WASTWATER

In an area noted for big deep waters, remote Wastwater stands out as the most forbidding example. With an **average** depth of over 120ft sloping down to a maximum 260ft, this is Englands deepest lake. And in truth, this most rugged of the Lakes is better noted for this fact than the quality of the fishing it provides.

The main species is brown trout. As you might expect if you don't know what you are doing, it would be quite easy for lures or baits to get lost in such a volume of water. Your best bet would generally be to ignore the really deep water and look for some of the shallower bays where you will find depths of a manageable fifteen to twenty feet, and where much of the trout's food will be found. Some of the shallows where the mountain streams enter the lake should also be examined.

The deeper water is the province of the charr. Not as productive as Windermere or Coniston, they can be caught in small numbers at various times of the year, but if you only have a short time in which to catch this colourful species then nearby Ennerdale would possibly be a better bet.

The River Irt flows out of the western end of the lake towards the Irish Sea and a modest run of salmon and sea trout ascend into the lake to spawn but few fish are caught in the lake itself. (For River Irt details see rivers section).

The coarse fish of Wastwater present more of a mystery, the lake is said to contain both pike and perch, but few perch are caught and even fewer pike are reported. Having never caught either species from the lake, we can't really comment on this, but if you want to try, we would suggest you go to the areas where the trout are caught. Wherever there are trout, pike, and to a lesser extent perch, should not be far behind. Like most of the big lakes it fishes best for all species in the summer months.

The A595 is the nearest major road, with minor roads leading to the lakeside from Gosforth and Gubbergill. From central Lakeland the quickest route is over the Wrynose and Hard Knott Passes. At the time of writing day permits are not available for this water, but enquire at the National Trust campsite for further details.

WATENDLATH TARN

An increasing number of the more accessible Lakeland hill tarns are being given over to the stocking of commercially reared rainbow trout. A good example is Watendlath. Formerly a free fishery containing small brown trout, perch and pike, the tarn is now stocked with brown and rainbow trout. Day and evening permits are available for the water, with four and two fish bag limits respectively.

To reach the water, take the B5289 out of Keswick. About two and a half miles along this road there is a smaller road going left to Watendlath village and the tarn is by this village. For further details about the water contact Mr. Stan Edmondson, Borrowdale Fisheries, Borrowdale, telephone 293.

WET SLEDDALE RESERVOIR

This small water supply reservoir two miles west of Shap can be fished on a day permit available from the Bampton Post Office, near the water. The water is fly only for brown trout. At the time of going to press, a number of changes were being made to many reservoirs under the control of the NWWA, and permit details may have changed by the time you read this, so don't take these facts as gospel!

WHINFELL TARN

Lying amongst the lush farmlands of southern lakeland, this small eight acre tarn is stocked with perch, rudd, roach, tench, pike and eels. It's a rich little water and the fish, particularly the rudd, seem to thrive. Only part of the banking may be fished and permission to do so must first be sought from the farm house near the tarn. It can be found to the north east of Kendal, just off the A685 turning towards Grisdale at the village of Grayrigg.

WHINS POND

This twenty acre water used to be run as a trout fishery until recently (1989), now the waters stocks include roach, bream, tench, carp, rudd, perch and some chub and trout. Tickets are available from the house overlooking the pond from 7.00 a.m. and must be obtained before fishing, matches can also be booked, contact Mrs. E. Siddle, Penrith 62671.

Situated near Penrith, the fishery is easy to locate from the M6 at junction 40. From here take the A686 towards Edenhall, on the right of this road you will see a turn off to Honey Pot Farm, the water is down this road.

WINDERMERE

Still often described as the "Queen of the Lakes", unfortunately for England's longest lake her crown has become a little tarnished these days, for this ten mile long water is easily the most commercialised of the big Cumbrian Lakes. With hundreds of reclining sunbathers lining the more accessible parts of the shoreline — the blare of transistor radios competing with the delighted cries of swimmers — Windermere at the height of the holiday season will hardly seem the stuff of which angling dreams are made. All this would not be so bad if these noisy activities were confined to the shore, but this lake is also a haven for water skiers who have been effectively denied the use of all the other lakes in the area — and they take full advantage of the fact.

Surprisingly, despite all these encroachments, sport on this still beautiful lake can be good, if not at times, excellent.

Certainly for top quality brown trout fishing, Windermere still reigns supreme among the big Cumbrian Lakes. Indeed,

WINDERMERE
(DEPTHS IN METRES)

for completely natural brown trout fishing few waters in the country can compare with Windermere. Most good bags of fish average between ten ounces to one and a quarter pounds but there are also bigger fish taken. Fish up to four pounds are caught on a fairly regular basis.

For most practical purposes the lake is almost divided in two by the large wooded Belle Isle and most Windermere regulars refer to fishing in either the northern or the southern basins, almost as if they were talking of two separate lakes. The southern part of the lake is generally shallower than that of the north and most of the better trout catches seem to come from this area. Unlike many of the other Cumbrian lakes, Windermere can fish well for trout from 15th March when the season starts, right through to late July; the shores around the lake's several large and small islands are noted hot spots and these will best be fished from a boat. Indeed, although bank fishing can be practised, most anglers take to a boat in this lake, and the majority of the better catches come to the angler afloat.

Although some very big pike were once caught from this lake, including fish up to thirty pounds, the situation now seems to be much less hopeful. This is in no small part due to the operations of the Windermere-based Freshwater Biological Association who regularly net the pike population for research. So nowadays you will be lucky to find fish above five or six pounds. However, recent reports suggest that some fairly big pike still exist in the lake, double figure specimens up to eighteen pounds have been reliably reported by the few anglers pike fishing there, and certainly there is such a volume of water facing the angler that some bigger pike must still be present. If you want to try, Belle Isle and the waters off Wray Castle in the northern basin should be worthwhile, but really Windermere is such a massive and feature-packed piece of water that the visitor will find many other "pikey" looking spots along its shoreline. Again, like the trout angler, a boat is an excellent way of exploring the lake.

The perch seem to be recovering from the disease which decimated their numbers several years ago. Quite a few fish in the one pound to one and a half pound range are starting to be caught again. The area around the ferry crossing (close to where the F.B.A have their headquarters) is worth a try. Spinning in the shallows at the lake's southern end, around where the River Leven leaves the lake, will probably also turn up plenty of perch and trout. The lake is also teeming with eels in the summer and good catches are made in the shallower weedy bays.

Windermere is also home to the charr, a fish we have already encountered earlier in the book when discussing the potential of waters like Coniston and Ennerdale amongst others. With the possible exception of Coniston, this is one of the most important venues for the species, and the tradition of charr fishing on the lake goes back hundreds of years. Traditional tackle is still used, in fact; if you visit Windermere between May and October you might be

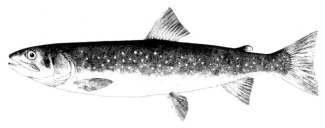

Charr

puzzled by the sight of rowing boats equipped with two long bamboo poles protruding from either side of the boat. This method of charr fishing has been practised for over 150 years and involves the slow trolling of several small shiny spoons set at various depths to catch this much sought after delicacy. It is called plumb lining because of the large plumb weight used at the end of the line and a skilled practitioner can catch many fish during a days trolling, ranging from six ounces up to nearly a pound. Most of the charr are fished for and caught in the northern basin, and the best chance a visiting angler has of encountering this beautiful fish is by trolling the deeper water with a small mepps spinner or similar shiny lure.

The season for charr is from May 1st to October 31st, but the most productive times are usually betwen May and August. You would be advised to make an early start at this time of year because of the speedboats.

The fishing for all the species in the lake is free, providing the relevant NWWA rod permit has been bought. However, a lot of the banking is in private hands and that is one of the reasons why we suggest a boat as the best means of fishing the lake. You can either hire a rowing boat from the many centres around Ambleside and Bowness or you can launch your own. There are three public launching sites dotted along the eastern shoreline; one at Ambleside on the northern tip of the lake, another in the middle part of the lake near Bowness and a smaller facility further south near Storrs.

Wigan and District Angling Association also control five miles of banking on the Graythwaite Estates along the lake's western shore; for details of this Association contact Mr. W. Gratton, 55 Balcarres Road, Aspull, Wigan, telephone 831290.

YEW TREE TARN

A water specially created in the 1930's as a fishing venue, situated along the main A593 between Coniston village and Skelwith Bridge. The tarn is now under the control of the Coniston and Torver Angling Association and contains brown and rainbow trout. Day tickets are available from Coniston Gifts and Sports Shop in Coniston; the shop is easy to find, being directly opposite the large car park in the village.

NOTES:

LAKELAND RIVERS

AIRA BECK

Rising around Matterdale Common and running into the south western corner of Ullswater, the beck offers a limited amount of small stream trout fishing. The better sport is generally to be found in the lower reaches, near to the confluence with the lake. Most of the beck runs through National Trust property and the fishing is free. There is good access to the lower reaches from either the A595 or the A5091. The spectacular Aira Force waterfall is one of Cumbria's biggest tourist attractions and is certainly worth a look if you are in the area.

RIVER ANNAS

A small river running off Bootle Fell in the south west corner of the district, very much off the "tourist trail" and well worth a visit. The river rarely attains any great size but nonetheless offers some reasonable game fishing opportunities. The brown trout are plentiful along much of the river's three mile course although they rarely attain any great size and there is also a modest run of sea trout; both species tend to be late running and few are caught before June.

Most of the best fishing is concentrated in the river's last two miles. This is under the control of Millom & District A.A. Although there are no day permits available, full club membership may be obtained from the Secretary, at 19 Market Street, Millom, Cumbria.

RIVER BELA

Located in the most southerly part of Cumbria, the Bela is formed by the conjunction of two small streams. Close to the village of Crooklands the enlarged Bela then flows a further three miles before emptying into the eastern corner of the River Kent estuary.

A fairly rich environment provides one of the southern area's better brown trout fisheries. Unfortunately, much of the best reaches are in private hands and there are few openings for the individual visitor. Your best bet will be to try local landowners around Milnthorpe for permission. Milnthorpe A.A. also controls some stretches of the river along with a number of other smaller becks.

RIVER BRATHAY

The Brathay has its source high in the Langdales from where it flows through the Wrynose Pass before entering Little Langdale Tarn. In these upper reaches the water is little more than a typical mountain stream and will be of limited interest to the majority of anglers. However, a much enlarged river flows out of the tarn and on to its second meeting with a major waterway, when its waters join with those of Elter Water. Below this point much of the best fishing is concentrated. The river finally flows into the northern tip of Lake Windermere.

A very interesting water to fish, particularly around Skelwith Bridge, the Lower Brathay is best known for brown trout. There is a two mile stretch of water under the control of Windermere and District A.A. This is located in the very lowest reaches between Windermere and Jiffy Knotts Wood; permits are widely available at most tackle shops and Tourist Information Offices in the area. Permission to fish other reaches of the river must be obtained from landowners. Charr are sometimes reported in this river when they enter the water from Windermere to spawn.

RIVER CALDER

A river of about seven miles, it rises on Stockgill Moor, from where it flows due west before emptying into the Irish Sea in the shadow of the (in)famous Sellafield nuclear reprocessing plant. The river offers some good brown trout fishing; salmon and sea trout also run from July through to September. Calder A.A. have a good deal of the better fishing as well as fishing on Wormgill, one of the river's main tributaries.

The Association make only a very limited number of visitor's season tickets available. Applications must be made by post to The Secretary, Calder A.A., 10/24 The Knoll, Egremont, Cumbria.

RIVER COCKER

Fed by the waters of Buttermere, Crummock and Loweswater from where it flows north to its confluence with the River Derwent on the northern outskirts of Cockermouth, this is one of the Derwents most important tributaries, containing brown trout in abundance and with substantial runs of salmon and sea trout. These two last species are usually at their most prolific in the latter part of the year, the salmon from late October to late November and the sea trout finding August onwards more to their liking. Cockermouth A.A. offer tickets on their stretches of the river and these are available from The Gun Shop, Lorton Street, Cockermouth, telephone 822058.

The National Trust has some water on this river, for further information enquire at their shop (Wordsworth House) in Cockermouth, telephone 824805. Otherwise there are few openings for the visiting angler. Your best bet would be to try local land owners along the B5289 and the road along the other side of the river for permission to fish. May is one of the best months for brown trout.

RIVER CRAKE

Flowing out of the southern tip of Coniston at High Nibthwaite and reaching its estuary at Greenodd four miles further south, this short river is best known as a brown trout fishery. However, salmon and sea trout enter into Coniston Lake via this river and fishing for them can be quite productive at times, from July onwards. Night or late evening fishing is particularly productive for all species on this river. There are also small numbers of coarse fish in the form of a few pike and perch.

Ulverston Angling Association control the fishing rights to some parts of the river. However, the Association limit the fishery to members only. There is some accessible fishing at Lowick Farm, Lowick Bridge where day tickets are issued by the farm.

CRUMMOCK BECK

A tributary of the River Waver and absolutely nothing to do with Crummock Water, it is not a particularly important fishery, just a few brown trout in the lower reaches before entering the main river at Abbey Town. Some polite enquiries to local farmers will probably be all you need to fish the beck.

RIVER DERWENT including River Greta, River Marron

One of Cumbria's most important river systems, the Derwent has its source at Scafell from where it flows through the Borrowdale Valley, passing into Derwentwater and Bassenthwaite before emptying into the Irish Sea at Workington, a distance of around thirty miles.

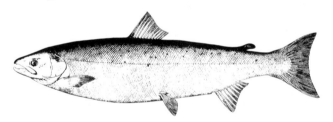

Salmon

The salmon fishing is good, in fact, at the right time excellent sport can be had with fish up to and over twenty pounds being encountered in most good seasons. The salmon fishing seems to be at its best between July through to September, although late October will still see plenty of fish in the river in a good season. The sea trout are also well represented, July and August generally being the best months. One particularly encouraging aspect of the Derwent is the even spread of the fish and they can be encountered in most reasonable stretches of the river when they are running.

The brown trout fishing can also be very good. Most of the fish average around half a pound but can attain a greater size than this in the better reaches, particularly those lower down the river.

Pike are also present in the deeper, slower-moving parts of the river, but like many river pike, they are relatively untouched by the serious angler; however, fish up to twenty eight pounds have been reported so the potential is obviously there.

Although some of the fishing on the river is in private hands there are some fairly accessible reaches. For example, Keswick A.A. have the fishing rights on the river between Derwentwater and Bassenthwaite. Permits must be obtained by post from W. Ashcroft, Springhaven, How Lane, Portinscale, Keswick (enclose a stamped addressed envelope).

A good deal of the fishing on the river running out of Bassenthwaite's northern end is under the control of Castle Fisheries, who issue a limited number of permits for salmon, sea trout and brown trout. These can be obtained from Mr. S. G. Payne, Fishery Manager, Cockermouth Castle, Cockermouth, telephone 826320 or The Tackle Shop, Helvellyn Street, Keswick. In the lower reaches of the river Workington A.A. are the main holders of fishing rights, but their beats are generally limited to members and their guests.

Apart from the River Cocker (see previous page) the other two main tributaries of the Derwent are the River Greta and the River Marron. The River Greta enters the main river just west of Keswick, and much of the information concerning the main river can also apply to this fishery but on a much smaller scale. The salmon and sea trout are less numerous and the brown trout are much smaller. The main fishing holders are Keswick A.A., and permit details are as for the main river.

The River Marron enters the Derwent further downstream at the village of Bridgefoot. The fishing on this minor river is mainly confined to small brown trout, although a few sea trout can be found in a spate. Branthwaite Mill, Branthwaite, offers some fishing on the middle reaches.

Other smaller becks within the Derwent system which offer a limited amount of free fishing for brown trout include the higher reaches of the Derwent itself, which is also joined by Stonethwaite Beck at Rosthwaite and Naddle Beck near Keswick. There are also Coldale and Newlands Becks; these two small waters join together and flow adjacent to the Derwent for a couple of miles before entering Bassenthwaite Lake at the lake's south western corner. Also St. John's Beck which joins the Greta at Threlkeld, and finally the River Glenderamakin close to the A66, which picks up the tiny Mosedale Beck before continuing on to the River Greta. You will often find no problem gaining access to these little waters, but even so, do ask permission first.

RIVER DUDDON including River Lickle

On its journey down the Wrynose Pass in southern Cumbria, the Duddon picks up the majority of its feeder streams from Ulpha and Seathwaite Fells; the enlarged river then flows in the southerly direction to its estuary a few miles north of Barrow-in-Furness. Most local anglers would be forced to agree that his little river is certainly not one of the most productive.

However, salmon, sea trout and brown trout are present and much of the fishing is controlled by Millom and District A.A. and is for members only. Apply to D. Dixon, 1 Churchill Drive, Millom, Cumbria.

The main tributary is the River Lickle, which flows from Broughton Moor and joins the Duddon just before it enters the sea. The river offers, principally, brown trout fishing but, like the main river, is not particularly productive. Two angling associations control water on the Lickle, Millom and District A.A. and also the Furness Fishing Association; day tickets for these associations' waters are available from Hannay's Tackle Shop, Crellin Street, Barrow-in-Furness.

RIVER EDEN including River Caldew, River Eamont, River Irthing, River Leith, River Lowther, River Petterill.

The Eden is one river which will need little introduction to the dedicated game angler. Stretching from its source at Abbotside Common in North Yorkshire to its estuary seventy miles north west at Rockcliffe this is easily Cumbria's major river system.

As you might expect of such a large water, the fishing is highly variable from the delightful little trout stream above Kirkby Stephen to the wide and slower flowing deep pools nearer to Carlisle. The river is noted as a good game river with salmon ascending in the back end of the year and sea trout from June, July and August. The river is also home to a large number of coarse fish, the main species being chub, dace (present in truly vast numbers) as well as a smaller number of grayling. Unfortunately, these fish can only be fished for on a limited number of stretches, and often only during the salmon and sea trout close season.

Kirkby Stephen D.A.A. control just over twenty miles of the river in the higher reaches. This is fly only water. Although there is a waiting list for club membership, day tickets can be bought from Robinson's Toy Shop, Silver Street, Kirkby Stephen, telephone 71747.

Lower downstream a stretch of the river is controlled by the Appleby A.A. This is good trout water with fish averaging around half a pound along with some bigger samples up to two pounds plus, but this is available for members only. However, the Tufton Arms in Market Square, Boroughgate have some fly only water on the river for the exclusive use of their residents.

Much of the water as it flows just east of Penrith is under the control of Penrith A.A. The fishing around Little Salkeld and Bolton is open to visiting anglers and permits may be obtained from, C. R. Sykes, Tackle Shop, 4 Great Dockray, Penrith, Cumbria, telephone 62418. A little further downstream at Great Salkeld, The Highland Drove Residential Establishment offers a small portion of the river; for details telephone Lazonby 349.

Between Great Salkeld and Armathwaite, salmon and trout fishing water is owned by Bracken Bank Lodge,

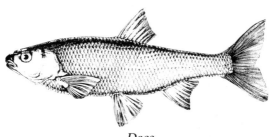

Dace

Lazonby, telephone Lazonby 241. Lazonby Estates provide some day tickets for spinning and fly fishing for salmon and trout, and they also allow coarse fishing during the winter months for species like chub and dace which swarm in most good stretches of the river. For details, apply to Lazonby Estates Office, Castlerigg Farm, Armathwaite, telephone Armathwaite 337.

The Fetherston Arms has a two mile stretch of river, for details contact Lazonby 284. Coarse fishing clubs can book a short but very productive length of river near Armathwaite, for further details telephone Mr. E. Ecroyd, Low House, telephone Armathwaite 242. This is a very popular piece of water with the coarse angler and only advance booking will get you on to the river.

Further down the river, a few miles south of Carlisle, there is a productive stretch under the control of Warwick Hall. For details of salmon and sea trout permits contact Mrs. Elwes, Warwick Hall, telephone Wetheral 60291. If you want to fish for brown trout, chub, dace or grayling then the man to contact is Mr. D. Haughin, Keeper's House, Warwick Hall, telephone Wetheral 60545.

In the lower reaches of the river, Carlisle A.A. control over seven miles of excellent fishing as well as part of the River Caldew, one of its tributaries. This provides good salmon and sea trout fishing in spring and autumn, coarse fish are also very well represented with large shoals of dace and chub. Permits and further information can be obtained from either McHardy's of Carlisle, South Henry Street, telephone 23988 or Carlisle Angling Centre, 105 Lowther Street, Carlisle, telephone 24035. Finally, there are weekly or daily permits for trout fishing issued by Dalston Parish Council, Dalston, Carlisle and Dalston Hall Caravan Site, telephone Dalston 71065.

Naturally, on such a long river, many tributaries join the Eden, both large and small. Here are a few of the more important fisheries.

The River Irthing flows in to the Eden just before Carlisle, Warwick Hall Estates own part of this river. They issue day tickets for salmon, sea trout, brown trout and coarse fishing (telephone Wetheral 60545). Both the trout and coarse fishing is excellent on these two stretches. Day tickets for trout and coarse fishing on this river and the River Gelt (another tributary) can be obtained from Atkinson's Sports Shop, Front Street, Brampton, telephone Brampton 3538.

The River Eamont, another major tributary, joins with the main river at Udford, a few miles east of Penrith, a distance of only six miles from its source at Ullswater. The grayling fishing on this river is particularly good, but brown trout are also well represented through most of the river's length, a few salmon trout and sea trout as well. Penrith A.A. are the major club water holders on this river, controlling a stretch from Pooley Bridge down to Yarwath Viaduct. Permits for all Penrith A.A. waters may be obtained from C. R. Sykes, 4 Great Dockray, Penrith, telephone Penrith 62418. The club also controls some fishing on the smaller River Petteril, permits are available from the same source.

RIVER EEA

A rather short, narrow river running through Cartmel and Cark in the southern part of the district, emptying into the Ulverston Channel on the northern edge of Morecambe Bay. The fishing is mainly confined to small brown trout, although the occasional sea trout is also reported from time-to-time. Cark and District A.A. control some of the fishing.

Contact Mr. G. Oliver, Fellside, Fern Hill Road, Grange-over-Sands, telephone 3445 for further details about membership.

RIVER EHEN

The Ehen flows from the western tip of Ennerdale Water, through Cleator Moor and around the outskirts of Egremont before sharing its estuary with the Calder close to Sellafield. The brown trout fishing is good along most of the river's ten miles; although the fish tend to be on the small side they are very free rising. Salmon and sea trout run up the river to spawn in the lake, these fish tend to make their presence felt around June through to August.

Some fishing in the upper reaches, from the lake's outflow down to Briscoe Bridge at Egremont, is under the control of Wath Brow and Ennerdale A.A. Permits can be obtained from Mr. E. Littlefaire, Wath Brow Post Office, Ennerdale Road, Cleator Moor or The Complete Angler, King Street, Whitehaven, telephone 5322.

RIVER ELLEN

Rising on Uldale Fells about four miles north east of Bassenthwaite from where it travels a distance of eighteen miles to its estuary at Maryport Harbour. Provides fairly good brown trout fishing, especially in the early summer. The salmon and sea trout ascend in only moderate numbers, June, July and August being the most likely time to contact a fish.

Aspatria A.C. have some fishing on the river, permits for which are available from R. and J. Holt, Outgang Road, Aspatria; lower down the river, Ellen A.A.make both season and day tickets available from R. Thompson, 127 Crosby Street, Maryport, telephone 812310.

RIVER ESK

The Esk starts its journey around the area of Scafell Pike, being very close to the source of the River Derwent which flows in the opposite direction. As it makes its way to the sea at Ravenglass, the river passes through some beautiful countryside, making this one of the loveliest to fish in the whole area.

Provides fairly good salmon and sea trout fishing at the right time of year, with June and July usually being the best months. There is also a good stock of brown trout.

Eskdale Estates issue a few day permits for all three species, in the lower parts of the river around Ravenglass and these can be obtained from The Pennington Arms Hotel, Ravenglass, telephone 222. Millom and District A.A. have some fishing available on the Esk, but this is for members only. For membership apply to D. J. Dixon, 1 Churchill Drive, Millom, Cumbria (enclose a stamped addressed envelope with all correspondence).

Geoff Parkinson with two good conditioned Lakeland pike caught within a minute of each other by the authors.

RIVER GILPIN

The source of the Gilpin is in Gilpin Park Plantation, not far from Windermere, from here it makes its way to the Kent estuary via Crosthwaite and down the Lyth Valley to Sampool. The main species are brown trout with some sea trout and a few roach. Northern A.A. control a short length at Crosthwaite and permits are available from most local tackle shops in Kendal. Some riparian owners give permission to fish the river as it flows through their land, provided permission is sought **first.**

GOLDRILL and GRISEDALE BECKS

Two small and somewhat insignificant fisheries. The Goldrill is the small stream connecting Brothers Water with Ullswater and Grisedale Beck is its only tributary. Both offer free fishing for brown trout.

GRIZEDALE BECK (RUSLAND POOL)

A tributary of the River Leven, Grizedale Beck starts its life in the Grizedale Forest which is situated between Lakes Coniston and Windermere. From here it flows in a southerly direction and from the village of Rusland the beck changes its name to Rusland Pool before joining with the Leven at Haverthwaite.

The main species are brown trout with a few sea trout making the journey into the lower reaches of the river. The beck flowing through Grizedale Forest is controlled by The Forestry Commission and permits can be obtained from the Camp Warden, Ambleside, or by post from The Forestry Commission Offices, Grizedale, Ambleside, telephone Satterthwaite 373.

Gaining permission to fish on the generally more desirable Rusland Pool will be a lot trickier and there seem to be few if any real openings for the visiting angler. Try the old trick of asking local landowners.

RIVER IRT including River Bleng

Best known as a sea trout and salmon fishery, one of the better "smaller" rivers for this species in Cumbria. The river is an outflow of Wastwater from where it flows west to its estuary at Drigg, a distance of some ten miles. July and August are usually the best months for the sea trout and salmon with the brown trout being at their best through most of the summer.

Permits for over three and a half miles are available for residents of the Lutwidge Arms Hotel, Holmrook, telephone 230. However, a limited number of weekly and day tickets are also available for non-residents. Millom and District A.A. control some of this river although no day permits are issued and it is reserved for members only, for details see entry on River Esk.

Gosforth A.A. also control a short stretch of the river, three miles in all, around Wasdale in the upper reaches, and this is for members only.

The River Bleng is the only major tributary of any consequence, with some of the fishing controlled by Millom and District. Although the salmon and sea trout are less numerous, much of what has been said about the main river can be applied. In the upper reaches, some riparian owners will allow fishing if asked.

RIVER KENT including River Gowan, River Mint, River Sprint

The Kent flows from Kentmere Reservoir, which is situated about six miles north of Staveley on Kentmere Common. At Staveley it is joined by the smaller River Gowan, which flows from Borrans Reservoir, four miles to the west. The next major tributary, the River Sprint, is joined at Burneside and a further mile downstream the River Mint is the river's only other main tributary.

Surprisingly, this beautifully situated river has been no stranger to pollution. The most recent case happened when a small quantity of cyanide was released into the river on the outskirts of Kendal. Happily, this incident has not led to the total devastation that many predicted and the Kent, along with its smaller tributaries, is still able to offer the angler some top quality game fishing. The river is best known as a brown trout fishery, and this fish is present in good numbers along most reasonable stretches of the system. Fish up to a pound are a fairly regular feature of catches, and a few fish up to five pounds plus are reported from time to time. The trout on the Mint and the Sprint are equally numerous but tend to be quite a bit smaller, with fish of over half a pound being the exception.

The river also offers some productive salmon and sea trout fishing. Generally speaking this is thought of as a "late" river; although a few fish make their appearance in the spring, they are not present in any great quantity until the end of August.

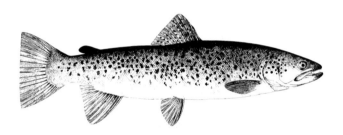

Brown Trout

Fortunately, there are quite a few stretches of the river open to the visiting angler. In the higher reaches, around Staveley, the river is controlled by Staveley Angling Association, who issue weekly permits. These can be obtained from D. and H. Woof, Newsagents, 22 Main Street, Staveley, telephone 821253. This permit will also cover the Association's fishing on the nearby River Gowan. The trout tend to be smaller in these upper reaches, but they are fairly numerous.

Burneside and District A.A. have two and a half miles of banking on part of the main river, stretching from Staveley sewage works down to Eggholme Wood. Permits can be obtained from The Jolly Anglers Inn, Burneside, telephone Kendal 24020. The Association also controls some fishing on the River Sprint around Sprint Bridge.

Kent Angling Association are the major water holders on the lower reaches of the river, both above and below Kendal. Day and weekly permits can be obtained from Kendal Sports Shop, 30 Stramongate, Kendal, telephone 21554. Fly fishing, spinning and worm fishing is allowed around here, and this part of the river is one of the better bets if salmon and sea trout are your principal prey. There is also some free fishing in the river where it flows through Kendal, for details check at the Tourist Information Offices within the town, but don't forget to buy the appropriate rod licence.

Day tickets for fishing on the Kent near Sedgwick are available from the Site Manager, Low Park Wood Caravan Site, Sedgwick. Lower down from Sedgwick, below Levens Bridge, this section of the river is tidal, but there is some good fishing available at Sampool, for details contact, Mr. L. Parsons, Lower Leven Farm, Kendal, telephone 60435. Finally, if you are into sea fishing then the Kent estuary offers some of the most productive flounder fishing in the country — just a thought!

KIRKBY POOL

Furness Fishing Association (Game Section) control the fishing on this small beck which enters the sea at Kirkby-in-Furness. Game section permits are available from Hannay's Tackle Shop, Crellin Street, Barrow-in-Furness, telephone 22571. A very small number of salmon and sea trout run up this beck, but the main species is small brown trout.

RIVER LEVEN

The Leven flows from the southern tip of Lake Windermere, passing through Newby Bridge to the sea at Greenodd a distance of some four and a half miles. This is quite a substantial river and provides some first class fishing for salmon, sea trout and brown trout. There are also a few coarse fish (pike and perch) in the upper reaches as it leaves the lake.

In fact, such is the quality of the game fishing that there are almost no openings for the visiting angler. The only available permits can be obtained for a short stretch opposite the Swan Hotel, Newby Bridge, telephone 31681. This is rather a popular spot with our old friends, the tourists, and is also more than a little crowded with boats. Pick your fishing times with extreme care.

RIVER LUNE including River Rawthey

Has its source on Ravenstonedale Common some five miles south west of Kirkby Stephen. From here this famous northern salmon river flows south, through Tebay and Kirkby Lonsdale before reaching the sea at Lancaster, a total distance of some forty-five miles. Few rivers can match its beauty and from the game anglers point of view this is one of the areas most important rivers. Although the habits of both species of fish in recent years tend to suggest a change in the pattern, the river is still usually at its best for both species between August and September. The sea trout start showing in good numbers earlier and the month of June will usually see this species ascending the river in sizeable numbers.

In the upper reaches, the brown trout fishing can also be very productive, with good bags of fish taken in most of these stretches, particularly between the months of August to September. The river around Tebay down to below Kirkby Lonsdale is usually well stocked with this species and they tend to increase in size around the latter venue, where the river widens and deepens.

A great deal of the higher reaches are controlled by Tebay Fishing Club — a total of seventeen miles. The club issue a number of weekly tickets, but only to those anglers staying in the immediate area. For further details contact the Junction Hotel, Tebay, telephone Orton 232. Sedbergh Angling Association also issue weekly tickets, covering part of the Lune as well as substantial parts of the River Rawthey, which joins with the Lune below Sedbergh and these can be obtained from Lowis's, 45 Main Street, Sedbergh. A limited number of weekly tickets are issued.

Kirkby Lonsdale hold some very good fishing on the river between Barbon and Kirkby Lonsdale. The brown trout are well stocked, with a high average weight. The club issue a number of visitor's tickets, but these are only valid between Monday to Friday and are only sold to people staying locally (campers and caravans excluded). They are available from Kirkby Lonsdale at The Tackle Box, Kirkby Lonsdale, telephone 71663 or L. Barrie, Gent's Outfitter, Old Market Hall, Kirkby Lonsdale, telephone 71009.

RIVER LYNE

A tributary of the Border Esk and located in the far northern reaches of Cumbria, this small river rises in the Kielder Forest and joins the Border Esk a little downstream of the village of Longtown.

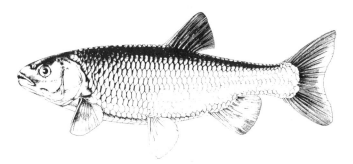

Chub

The river is known chiefly as a good chub fishing venue and the best fishing is to be had in the winter months when the river is less choked by weed. One of the most accessible stretches is located close to the A7 at Westlinton, where the road crosses the river. Permits for this part of the river may be obtained from A. E. Tuddenham, 21 Netherby Street, Longtown, telephone Longtown 273. Most chub caught are around one to two pounds in weight but some real specimens have been reported in previous seasons.

RIVER ROTHAY

This small river initially feeds the northern tip of Grasmere, flowing out of the southern end a much enlarged water. About half a mile downstream, the river has its second meeting with a lake when it joins with Rydal Water before completing its short journey to Lake Windermere a further one and a half miles away.

Pike

The best fishing is in the small stretch between Grasmere and Rydal, which provides fairly good, if unspectacular, brown trout fishing. There are perch and a few pike present too in the deeper slower moving parts. Windermere and District A.A. control this part of the river and day tickets are available from Broadgate's Newsagent, Grasmere or most Tourist Information Centres in the area. Canoes are becoming a big problem on this river.

TROUTBECK

The beck starts its short journey to Lake Windermere on Caudale Moor, over-shadowed by Stoney Cove Peak (2,502ft) and Thornthwaite Crag. Access to the beck is good, from the A592 Bowness to Patterdale road; it also flows under the A591, before entering Lake Windermere about one mile north of Calgarth Hall on the eastern side of the lake.

In the lower reaches some perch are present, but the main species is the brown trout. Windermere D.A.A. control fishing on part of the beck and permits for their waters are issued by local Tourist Information Centres in Ambleside and Windermere.

RIVER WAMPOOL

More of a beck than a real river actually. It starts its short life around Wigton in the far north western corner of the county and from here it flows for six miles to the Solway Firth at Kirkbride, emptying into Moricambe Bay. The main species is the brown trout and a few sea trout can sometimes be encountered in the very lowest reaches. Anglers wishing to fish this river should ask locally; most of the fishing is free, but it does pay to ask first.

WATENDLATH BECK

Situated about two miles south of Derwentwater, the beck drains from Watendlath Tarn and into Derwentwater, near the Lodore Hotel at the southern end of the lake. The fishing is free and brown trout is the only anglers' species present.

RIVER WINSTER

The source of this small river is to be found two miles south of Bowness, from where it follows the old boundary between Lancashire and Cumbria over Cartmel Fell before entering Morecambe Bay, very close to Lindale on the A590. Species present are sea trout, salmon and brown trout. This is an unusually sluggish river for much of its length and coarse fish like roach, perch and even pike are to be found in the deeper lower parts of the river.

Wigan and District Angling Association control some fishing near the Little Chef at Lindale. For permit advice contact their Secretary, Mr. W. Gratton, 66 Balcarres Road, Aspull, Wigan, telephone Wigan 831290 or telephone their Membership Secretary Mr. K. Hogg on Wigan 492376. Some riparian owners also allow fishing in the higher reaches.

RATHER HEATH TARN

This quaint tarn of some four acres has recently been taken over by Windermere, Ambleside and District A.A. who make day tickets available from tackle shops and Tourist Information Centres, and must be obtained in advance.

Generally, the fishery is relatively shallow and weedy, which has provided an excellent environment for the many tench that inhabit the water. At present the club are carrying out a stocking policy which includes bigger tench and some rudd and roach, also present are gudgeon and some bream.

To find, take the first left to Crook off the A591 Kendal to Windermere road after the roundabout where the A5284 from Kendal meets the A591. The Tarn is a little way down this road on the right.

Other Castabout Guides currently available in the series:

Anglers' Guide to Lancashire

Anglers' Guide to North Yorkshire

Anglers' Guide to Dumfries and Galloway

Anglers' Guide to Durham and Cleveland

Anglers' Guide to Northumberland and Tyne and Wear

REVIEWS OF THE FIRST EDITION

"LAKE DISTRICT GUIDE A MUST — As well as covering all the famous big lakes and the less well known still water, the guide also includes an extensive section on the Lakeland rivers right up to the Eden in the far north."
Lancashire Evening Post

"WHAT'S YOUR LINE IN LAKELAND FISHING? — Which waters can I fish? What species are in them? What size are they? Where do I get permission to fish? I have often thought that a really detailed angling guide to Cumbria was long overdue. So much so that I decided to do something positive about this need. I wrote one!"   *James Holgate Lakescene*

"WHERE TO FIND THE DRUNKEN DUCK — Answering queries about fishing in the Lake District will be simple in future because north west anglers James Holgate and Geoff Parkinson have produced a comprehensive guide to every water — including Drunken Duck Tarn!"
Anglers' Mail

"LOCH, STOCK AND BARREL — a bargain not to be missed."   *West Lancashire Evening Gazette.*

"LAKELAND CASTS — For years I searched in vain for an accurate guide to Lakeland fishing. Put the flags out, I have found one at last, and it's cheap at the price. Entitled Lakeland Castabout, it is packed with up-to-date information."   *Daily Express*

"GOOD GUIDE TO LAKE FISHING — It is an accurate look at the angling potential of an area which boasts some of the biggest, longest and deepest lakes in the country. In the same series, the Castabout Guide to Dumfries and Galloway is equally useful and informative."   *Sheffield Morning Telegraph*

"FINE GUIDE TO LAKE DISTRICT — The potential of every water is mentioned, including species and the size the fish run to, together with information on where to obtain permits, where applicable."   *Coarse Angler*

A NEW GUIDE FOR LAKES ANGLERS — A new comprehensive guide to fishing in the Lake District"
Lancashire Clarion

NOTES: